Anne Lindsay's
New Light Cooking

by Anne Lindsay

In co-operation with
Denise Beatty, RD,
and the
Canadian Medical Association

ASSOCIATION **C** CANADIAN
MÉDICALE MEDICAL
CANADIENNE ASSOCIATION

Random House Canada

To my children, Jeff, John and Susie, with love.

Reprinted by Random House Canada, 2006

Nutrition information provided by Denise Beatty, RD.

First published in Canada by Ballantine Books,
a division of Random House of Canada, Toronto.

www.randomhouse.ca

Random House Canada and colophon are trademarks.

Library and Archives Canada Cataloguing in Publication
Lindsay, Anne 1943–
Anne Lindsay's New light cooking / in cooperation with Denise Beatty and the Canadian Medical Association.
Includes indexes.
ISBN-13: 978-0-679-31488-2
ISBN-10: 0-679-31488-1
1. Low-fat diet—Recipes. 2. Nutrition—Popular works. I. Beatty, Denise II. Canadian Medical Association III. Title. IV. Title: New light cooking.
RM237.7.L57 2006   641.5'638   C2006-901751-4

Photography: Bradshaw Photography Inc.
Food Styling: Olga Truchan
Prop Styling: Janet Wakenshaw
Book Design: Dianne Eastman
Page Composition: Benny Lee / Richard Hunt

Printed and bound in China
10 9 8 7 6 5 4 3 2 1

Front cover: Penne with Sweet Red Peppers, Black Olives and Arugula (page 100)

Contents

Foreword

Good health begins with simple things. Every physician knows proper nutrition is a key to good health. That is why the Canadian Medical Association is so delighted to be associated with Anne Lindsay's *New Light Cooking*. We hope you will consider Anne's latest offering, which benefited from input by medical experts and nutritionists across the country, to be another sign of doctors' commitment to your health.

Helping patients live longer, healthier lives is the ultimate goal of every Canadian physician. This tremendous book is an attempt to answer some of the questions patients routinely ask us concerning nutrition and the food choices they should make. It not only answers your questions but helps you make tasty choices as well.

We are proud to add this book to our growing CMA library. We are sure you will find it a welcome — and delicious — addition to your kitchen.

Bon appétit!

Victor Dirnfeld, MD
President
Canadian Medical Association

President	*Medical Editor*	*Consultants*
Victor Dirnfeld, MD	Catherine Younger-Lewis, MD	Maryann Hopkins, BSP
		Diane Logan, MD
Secretary General	*Advisory Board*	Robert McKendry, MD
Léo-Paul Landry, MD	Susan I. Barr, PhD	W. Grant Thompson, MD
	Gregory P. Curnew, MD	
Director of Professional Development	Shajia Khan, MBBS	*Production Manager*
Stephen Prudhomme	Judith C. Kazimirski, MD	Deborah A. Rupert
	Cynthia Mannion, RN, MSc(A)	
Editor-in-chief	Suzanne Robinson, MSW	*Director, Marketing and Business*
John Hoey, MD		*Development*
		Ken Elsey

Canadian Medical Association
1867 Alta Vista Drive, Ottawa, Ontario K1G 3Y6
888-855-2555; fax 613-731-9102   www.cma.ca

Acknowledgments

With each cookbook I write, I'm asked, "What's different about this one?" Well, with this book, a great deal is new, including an association with the Canadian Medical Association and a new look that includes beautiful color on every page. But at the top of the list I would put a very special feeling of excitement and enthusiasm that has been present from the beginning when the Canadian Medical Association first spoke to me about combining our concerns for healthy eating into a new cookbook. The excitement accelerated when my terrific agent, Denise Schon, got involved, and it has picked up speed as each new person brought his or her own contribution to the project.

Writing a book like this involves dedication and enormous attention to detail. Many people have devoted huge amounts of time, enthusiasm and expertise to it, and I'm extremely grateful to all of them. They have all been a pleasure to work with.

I'd like to thank the Canadian Medical Association, especially the Advisory Board (listed in full on page iv), Steve Prudhomme, Dr. Catherine Younger-Lewis, Ken Elsey, Deborah Rupert, Nadine Mathieu and Christine Pollock, for their tremendous commitment to this book and its success; Denise Beatty, RD, for undertaking the difficult task of researching and writing the nutrition information found throughout the book; Shannon Graham, Daphna Rabinovitch, Heather Epp and Susan Pacaud, my wonderful recipe testers, for their creativity and patience especially when retesting and retesting; Doug Pepper at Random House, who loves food, cooking and publishing cookbooks, for generating so much excitement and for putting together a wonderful editorial and design team; Dianne Eastman, the art director, for making the book look so beautiful; Jennifer Glossop and Bev Renahan for their editorial expertise; Barbara Schon, indexer; everyone at Random House, including David Kent, Duncan Shields and his Ballantine sales team, Pat Cairns, Susan Roxborough, Jennifer Shepherd, Alan Terakawa, and Vicki Black; Barbara Selley, RD, for the nutrient analysis of the recipes; Katherine Yonker for the Canadian Diabetes Association Food Choice Values; Nancy Williams for running my office; Michael Levine, my lawyer; Angus Reid for the national poll asking what nutrition questions you have asked your doctor; photographers Doug Bradshaw and Josef Teschl, food stylist Olga Truchan and props co-ordinator Janet Wakenshaw, for the beautiful photographs.

And, as always, a huge thanks to my expert taster and wonderful husband, Bob, for his support, guidance, enthusiasm and love.

Introduction

Everyday, new research confirms that what we eat affects our health. Less fat lowers our chances of heart disease: more milk improves our chance of avoiding osteoporosis. The list goes on and on.

For years now I've been committed to finding ways to make healthy foods tasty, satisfying and easy to prepare. I was delighted, therefore, when the Canadian Medical Association, the most respected medical organization in the country, asked me to work with them to create a new cookbook that would provide more great recipes and up-to-date nutrition information that didn't require a doctorate to understand. Together we hoped to produce a book that would have a sound basis in scientific research but would also dispel the idea that healthy foods have to be bland and boring.

This book is the result of that collaboration. It includes a wealth of information and research on nutrition issues that registered dietitian Denise Beatty assembled and presented in manageable pieces that you will find throughout the book. Her choices are based partly on a survey the CMA and the 43,000 doctors it represents conducted, asking doctors what nutrition issues most concerned their patients.

What most concerns you? The CMA found that weight loss and blood cholesterol are two of the most pressing issues. Dietary supplements and nutrition for children were also of concern. In this book you'll find not only the most recent findings in these areas, but also delicious dishes that will help meet your goals or needs, whether they are losing weight or watching your salt intake.

Another poll, run by Angus Reid, asked Canadians what nutrition-related concerns they had raised with their doctor in the past year. Again cholesterol was a prime concern. Other popular topics were fats, dieting and weight loss, vitamins and minerals, fiber and diabetes. You'll find information on these topics throughout the book as well.

The prevention of disease is not our only goal here. Eating not only fuels the body; it provides pleasure and companionship — and the delight of new experiences. Everyone asks me how I keep coming up with new recipes. The answer, simply, is that it is what I love to do. I love creating new healthy dishes to feed my family and friends. I sometimes just take an old favorite like chocolate cake and find ways to make it healthier by reducing the amount of fat; I substitute oil and buttermilk for butter and increase the flavor by adding extra cocoa. That's how I came up with the recipe for Easy Chocolate Cake with Chocolate Buttermilk Icing on page 264. Sometimes I take flavor combinations I love — like lemon, coriander and coconut milk — and I try them out in new ways. The recipe for Thai Chicken Curry in Coconut Milk on page 164 is the result of such an exploration. And to meet the growing interest in vegetarian eating, I often experiment with meatless versions of curries, stews, pasta and burgers.

After all the mixing and cooking — and eating — recipes that are well received are tested again and again and eventually find their way into my books. First, however, they are checked for their nutrient content. You'll find this information accompanying each recipe. And in this book for the first time they are also assessed for their contribution to the Canada's Food Guide recommendations. Accompanying each recipe are symbols that tell you how many Canada's Food Guide servings the recipe contributes to your daily total. (See pages 2 and 293 for more information.)

As in my other books, the recipes here are quick and easy to prepare and use ingredients you can find in supermarkets everywhere. I hope that you will enjoy them as much as my family and I have, and that you will find in the nutrition information accompanying these recipes a resource that will lead you to good health and great eating.

Anne Lindsay

Healthy Eating: What's It All About?

Throughout this book we refer to healthy eating and a healthy eating pattern. This pattern is the starting point from which all nutrition-related advice is given. Whatever your specific goal — to have a healthy pregnancy, to raise healthy children, to live to an old age, to reduce your chance of developing colon cancer or to lower your blood pressure — you need to start from the basic healthy eating pattern, adjusting it to suit your particular needs.

A healthy eating pattern means building meals and snacks around foods that are low in fat but high in complex carbohydrates (starches), fiber, vitamins, minerals and natural plant chemicals known to benefit health.

A Healthy Eating Pattern: The Basics

Healthy eating means:

- eating more vegetables and fruit;
- eating more starchy foods like legumes (dried beans, peas and lentils), cereal, bread, pasta and rice;
- choosing whole grain foods such as whole wheat bread and brown rice as much as possible;
- eating smaller portions of meat and poultry, and eating fish more often;
- choosing low-fat milk products as much as possible;
- cutting back on foods high in fat, including butter, margarine, fast foods, snack foods, cookies and pastries, rich sauces and dressings;
- consuming alcohol, caffeine-containing beverages and highly salted foods in moderation.

In addition to the foods eaten, healthy eating means developing a healthy relationship with food. Eating should be enjoyable, not fraught with fear and guilt. Healthy eating also means eating in moderation, steering clear of fads and unfounded food claims, and knowing when and how to include favorite foods and treats without overdoing it or feeling guilty or remorseful.

Canada's Food Guide Simplifies Healthy Eating

Canada's Food Guide to Healthy Eating

Food Group	Range of Servings Needed Each Day
Grain Products	5 to 12
Vegetables & Fruit	5 to 10
Milk Products	2 to 4 (for adults)
Meat & Alternatives	2 to 3

Key to Canada's Food Guide Serving

= 1 serving of Grain Products

= 1 serving of Vegetables & Fruit

= 1 serving of Milk Products

= 1 serving of Meat & Alternatives

Canada's Food Guide to Healthy Eating (see following pages) simplifies healthy eating principles by organizing foods into four food groups and recommending the number and size of servings you need each day from each group.

The upper range of servings recommended for both Grain Products and Vegetables & Fruit often takes people by surprise. Don't panic at the thought of eating 12 servings of grain or 10 of fruits and vegetables each day. These higher ranges aren't meant for everyone. The number of servings right for you depends on various factors — your age, sex, body size, activity level and caloric needs. Women and children likely need less than teenage boys or people working in physically demanding jobs.

It is also difficult to tell what a recipe contributes to your overall nutrition needs as outlined in Canada's Food Guide to Healthy Eating. To help you, each recipe in this book is accompanied by a row of symbols that indicate the food groups and number of Canada's Food Guide servings provided by a serving of that recipe. If, for example, a recipe is accompanied by these symbols: **2** **1** , it means that one serving of that recipe will contribute 2 Grain Products and 1 Meat & Alternative servings to your daily total.

Nutrition in the News

These are exciting times in the ever-expanding field of nutrition. The sheer volume of information we receive daily can drive even the most health-conscious people crazy. However, as promising as each new discovery is, it is important to maintain a dose of healthy skepticism when applying these new findings to your own life. Scientific studies are works in progress, not absolute truths. Findings are tentative until the evidence becomes so overwhelming that they are widely accepted. A good strategy is to wait and not make changes based on the results of a single research study.

This book includes information and advice based on many of the more recent nutrition-related discoveries, but above all we stress the power and pleasure of healthy eating as the foundation of good health. Food itself is the only thing we know for sure will provide the natural mix of nutrients and other components known to promote good health, safely and without undue risk.

Health Canada   Santé Canada

CANADA'S
Food Guide
TO HEALTHY EATING

Enjoy a variety
of foods from each
group every day.

Choose lower-
fat foods
more often.

Grain Products
Choose whole grain
and enriched
products more often.

Vegetables & Fruit
Choose dark green
and orange vegeta-
bles and orange fruit
more often.

Milk Products
Choose lower-fat
milk products more
often.

Meat & Alternatives
Choose leaner meats,
poultry and fish, as well
as dried peas, beans and
lentils more often.

Canada

CANADA'S

Food Guide

TO HEALTHY EATING
FOR PEOPLE FOUR YEARS
AND OVER

Different People Need Different Amounts of Food

The amount of food you need every day from the 4 food groups and other foods depends on your age, body size, activity level, whether you are male or female and if you are pregnant or breast-feeding. That's why the Food Guide gives a lower and higher number of servings for each food group. For example, young children can choose the lower number of servings, while male teenagers can go to the higher number. Most other people can choose servings somewhere in between.

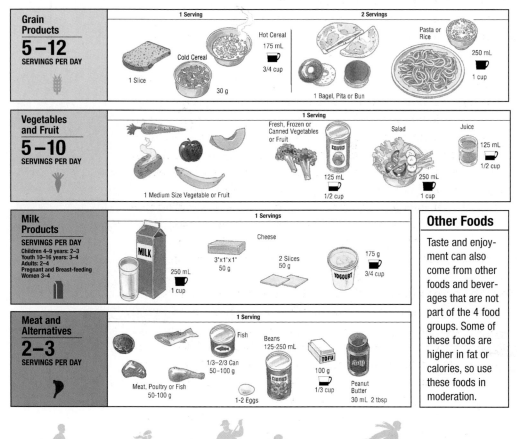

Grain Products

5 – 12

SERVINGS PER DAY

1 Serving — 1 Slice — Cold Cereal 30 g — Hot Cereal 175 mL 3/4 cup

2 Servings — 1 Bagel, Pita or Bun — Pasta or Rice 250 mL 1 cup

Vegetables and Fruit

5 – 10

SERVINGS PER DAY

1 Serving — 1 Medium Size Vegetable or Fruit — Fresh, Frozen or Canned Vegetables or Fruit 125 mL 1/2 cup — Salad 250 mL 1 cup — Juice 125 mL 1/2 cup

Milk Products

SERVINGS PER DAY
Children 4–9 years: 2–3
Youth 10–16 years: 3–4
Adults: 2–4
Pregnant and Breast-feeding Women 3–4

1 Servings — MILK 250 mL 1 cup — Cheese 3"x1"x1" 50 g — 2 Slices 50 g — 175 g 3/4 cup

Meat and Alternatives

2 – 3

SERVINGS PER DAY

1 Serving — Meat, Poultry or Fish 50-100 g — Fish 1/3–2/3 Can 50–100 g — 1-2 Eggs — Beans 125-250 mL 1/3 cup — TOFU 100 g — Peanut Butter 30 mL 2 tbsp

Other Foods

Taste and enjoyment can also come from other foods and beverages that are not part of the 4 food groups. Some of these foods are higher in fat or calories, so use these foods in moderation.

Enjoy eating well, being active and feeling good about yourself. That's VITALIT*

4

Changing for the Better

At some time or another we all face aspects of our lives we would like to change, such as quitting smoking or adopting healthier eating and cooking habits. These changes are frequently difficult to make, but knowing how other people make positive alterations in their lives can help us succeed.

According to the research of three clinical psychologists,* successful change unfolds through predictable stages, each of which involves different approaches, techniques and coping skills. Each stage is crucial for success. For instance, people who plunge unprepared into the fourth stage, Action, set themselves up for failure since they have not adequately readied themselves.

THE STAGES OF CHANGE

Stage 1 Precontemplation: At this stage you are not even thinking about change. A significant event — a fortieth birthday or a high school reunion or a health crisis — typically moves you to the next stage.

Stage 2 Contemplation: You acknowledge a problem exists but put off doing anything about it. If you are overweight, you might talk about your weight, read about weight loss or buy diet books but never quite get around to losing weight.

Stage 3 Preparation: You enter this stage when you begin to make a solid commitment to change. The focus switches from the problem to the solutions. Using the weight loss example, you might look for a weight loss program, talk to your doctor about a diet or purchase a cookbook like this one in anticipation of learning to cook in healthier ways.

Stage 4 Action: You purposefully modify your life and substitute healthy habits for poor ones. You join a weight loss program, read food labels, buy lower calorie foods, eat less, use recipes from a cookbook like this and become more physically active.

Stage 5 Maintenance: You enter the maintenance stage when you have accomplished the change you set out to make, when, for example, you have lost all the weight you set out to lose. The challenge then becomes to continue to manage your eating and activity patterns so you don't regain the weight.

Stage 6 Relapse: Relapse occurs if you abandon the new habit. It's quite common to cycle forward and backward through the stages. For instance, you may be doing well in the Action stage when a crisis in another area of your life shifts you back to the Contemplation stage. The key to recovering from the Relapse stage is to review the unsuccessful change attempt, learn from it and try again.

* Prochaska JO, Norcross JC, DiClemente CC. *Changing for Good: A Revolutionary Six-stage Program for Overcoming Bad Habits and Moving Your Life Positively Forward.* New York: Avon Books, 1994.

Appetizers

Grilled Quesadillas

Shrimp Quesadillas

Mini Phyllo Tart Shells

Mango Salsa in Mini Phyllo Tarts

Spicy Hummus

Caramelized Onion and Basil Dip

Creamy Crab Dip

Black Bean Dip with Veggie Topping

Creamy Coriander Mint Dip

Smoked Trout Spread

Herbed Yogurt-Cheese

Mushroom Bruschetta

Marinated Mussels

Crab Cakes

Spiced Shrimp

Hoisin Smoked-Turkey Spirals

Sesame Wasabi Spirals

Roasted Red Pepper and Arugula Spirals

Smoked Salmon and Cream Cheese Spirals

Teriyaki Chicken Bites

Citrus Mint Iced Tea

Nutrition Notes

Losing Weight: "Losing Weight in Good Health"

Heart Disease: "Take Healthy Eating to Heart"

Cancer: "Cancer and Healthy Eating"

Alcohol: "Wine, Whisky and Your Health"

Grilled Quesadillas

These make a terrific snack, lunch or light supper. You can substitute Cheddar cheese for the mozzarella. Serve with salsa.

Lower-Fat Version

Substitute 1 sweet green or yellow pepper, chopped, for the avocado. Fat is then reduced to 5 grams per serving.

1	small avocado	1
1	tomato, diced	1
1/2 cup	corn kernels	125 mL
1/4 cup	chopped canned green chilies or green onion	50 mL
1/4 tsp	salt	1 mL
Pinch	pepper	Pinch
8	flour tortillas (8 inch/20 cm)	8
1 cup	grated skim or part-skim mozzarella cheese	250 mL
1/3 cup	chopped fresh coriander (cilantro) or parsley	75 mL

1 Peel and pit avocado; place half in bowl and mash until smooth. Chop remaining half; stir into bowl along with tomato, corn, green chilies, salt and pepper.

2 Spread mixture evenly over half of each tortilla. Sprinkle cheese and coriander over mixture. Fold uncovered half over filling; gently press edges together.

3 In nonstick skillet or on grill over medium heat, cook quesadillas for 1-1/2 minutes until bottom is lightly browned. Turn and cook for 1-1/2 minutes or until filling is heated through and cheese is melted. *Makes 8 servings.*

Make ahead: Through step 2; cover and refrigerate for up to 4 hours.

Per serving:

calories	**217**
protein	**8 g**
total fat	**8 g**
saturated fat	2 g
cholesterol	8 mg
carbohydrate	**28 g**
dietary fiber	**2 g**
sodium	**424 mg**

R.D.I. Vit A 6%, E 4%, C 13%, Folate 10%, Ca 11%(124 mg), Iron 13%, Zinc 10%.

Canada's Food Guide Serving:

1½ 🌾 ½ 🥕 ¼ ▮

Shrimp Quesadillas

I love the fresh dill flavor here; however, chopped fresh basil or coriander also taste wonderful. If available, add a few spoonfuls of chopped mild green chilies. Serve these for lunch, as a first course or an hors d'oeuvre.

1 cup	grated skim (7% b.f.) or part-skim (15% b.f.) mozzarella cheese	250 mL
8	flour tortillas (8 inch/20 cm)	8
1/2 cup	diced tomato	125 mL
1/2 cup	salad shrimp (2 oz/60 g)	125 mL
1/2 cup	crumbled feta or firm goat cheese (chèvre)	125 mL
1/3 cup	chopped fresh dill	75 mL
1/4 cup	chopped red or green onion	50 mL
1/4 tsp	hot pepper sauce	1 mL

Serving Tip
Use a pizza cutter or long chef's knife to cut quesadillas into wedges.

1 Sprinkle half of the mozzarella evenly over half of each tortilla.

2 In small bowl, stir together tomato, shrimp, feta cheese, dill, onion and hot pepper sauce; spoon evenly over mozzarella. Top with remaining mozzarella. Fold uncovered half over filling; gently press edges together.

3 In large non-stick skillet over medium-high heat, cook quesadillas, two at a time, for 3 to 5 minutes or until bottom is lightly browned. Turn and cook until cheese is melted and bottom is lightly browned. Cut each into 3 wedges. *Makes 24 pieces.*

Make ahead: Through step 2, cover and refrigerate for up to 4 hours.

Per piece:

calories	**70**
protein	**4 g**
total fat	**2 g**
saturated fat	**1 g**
cholesterol	**9 mg**
carbohydrate	**8 g**
dietary fiber	**1 g**
sodium	**126 mg**

R.D.I. Vit A 2%, E 1%, C 2%, Folate 2%, Ca 5%(55 mg), Iron 4%, Zinc 4%.

Canada's Food Guide Serving:
½ 🌾 ¼ 🍗

Mini Phyllo Tart Shells

These phyllo pastry shells are very easy to make, keep for weeks and are wonderful hors d'oeuvres when filled. Basically, the shells are made of 4 thicknesses of phyllo stacked with a light brushing of melted butter between them and cut into 2-inch (5 cm) squares. Fill with Seafood Salad (page 231), Mango Salsa (opposite page), or Smoked Salmon (opposite page).

3	phyllo pastry sheets	3
4 tsp	butter, melted	20 mL

1 Lay one sheet of phyllo on work surface, keeping remainder covered to prevent drying out. Brush with butter; fold in half to measure 12 x 8 inches (30 x 20 cm). Brush top with butter; cut into 2-inch (5 cm) squares.

2 Stack squares on angle to make four thicknesses for each shell; press into tiny 1-1/2 inch (4 cm) tart cups.

3 Bake in 375°F (190°C) oven for 3 to 5 minutes or until golden brown. Let cool. *Makes 36 shells.*

Make ahead: Store in cookie tin or cardboard box in dry place for up to 1 month.

Per tart shell:

calories	10
protein	0 g
total fat	1 g
saturated fat	trace
cholesterol	1 mg
carbohydrate	1 g
sodium	14 mg

R.D.I. Iron 1%.

Mango Salsa in Mini Phyllo Tarts

This winning combination of paper-light buttery pastry shells with a juicy, fragrant filling is one of my favorite hors d'oeuvres.

1	mango, peeled and finely diced	1
1/2 cup	finely diced red onion	125 mL
1/2 cup	finely chopped sweet green pepper	125 mL
2 tbsp	fresh lemon or lime juice	25 mL
2 tbsp	finely chopped fresh coriander (cilantro) and/or mint	25 mL
1/4 tsp	each ground cumin and pepper	1 mL
30	Mini Phyllo Tart Shells (opposite page)	30

1 In small bowl, combine mango, onion, green pepper, lemon juice, coriander, cumin and pepper.

2 Spoon into tart shells. Serve immediately.

Makes 1-1/2 cups (375 mL) salsa and 30 pieces.

Make ahead: Through step 1, cover and refrigerate for up to 1 day.

Smoked Salmon with Lime-Ginger Mayonnaise in Mini Phyllo Tarts

Fill each tart shell with 1/2 tsp (2 mL) Lime Ginger Mayonnaise (page 205).
Top with 1 tsp (5 mL) smoked salmon bits; garnish with leaf of fresh coriander.

Per piece:

calories	17
protein	trace
total fat	1 g
saturated fat	trace
cholesterol	1 mg
carbohydrate	3 g
dietary fiber	trace
sodium	16 mg

R.D.I. Vit A 3%, E 1%, C 7%, Folate 1%, Ca 0%(2 mg), Iron 1%,

Spicy Hummus

*Serve this hummus as a dip for fresh vegetables or whole wheat pitas or
as a spread in sandwiches, bagels or pitas. Because hummus is so easy to make
at the last minute, I always keep a can of chick-peas in the cupboard.*

1	can (19 oz/540 mL) chick-peas, drained and rinsed	1
3 tbsp	each fresh lemon juice and water	50 mL
2	cloves garlic, minced	2
1 tbsp	sesame oil or 2 tbsp (25 mL) tahini or peanut butter	15 mL
1-1/2 tsp	ground cumin	7 mL
1/2 tsp	hot pepper sauce or cayenne pepper	2 mL
3 tbsp	chopped fresh parsley or coriander (cilantro)	50 mL
2 tbsp	chopped bottled jalapeño pepper (optional)	25 mL

I In food processor, purée chick-peas, lemon juice, water, garlic, sesame oil, cumin
and hot pepper sauce. (If too thick, add more water, 1 tbsp/15 mL at a time, until
hummus is a soft spreadable consistency.) Transfer to serving bowl. Sprinkle with
parsley, and jalapeño pepper (if using). *Makes about 2 cups (500 mL).*

Make ahead: Cover and refrigerate for up to 1 week.

Lemon-Dill Hummus: Increase lemon juice to 1/4 cup (50 mL). Omit sesame oil,
cumin, parsley and jalapeño pepper. Add 2 tbsp (25 mL) olive oil and 1/4 cup
(50 mL) packed chopped fresh dill and purée with chick-peas.

Sun-Dried Tomato Hummus: Pour 1/2 cup (125 mL) boiling water over 1/2 cup
(125 mL) dry-packed sun-dried tomatoes; let stand for 10 to 15 minutes or until
softened. Drain, saving liquid. Prepare Spicy Hummus, substituting 1/4 cup (50 mL)
soaking liquid for the water. Add half of the tomatoes to processor with chick-peas.
Add extra soaking liquid if processed mixture is too thick. Coarsely chop remaining
tomatoes and stir into hummus.

White Bean Hummus: Substitute 1 can (19 oz/540 mL) white kidney beans,
drained and rinsed, for the chick-peas. Omit jalapeño pepper.

Caramelized Onion and Basil Dip

Slowly cooked onions add a richness that complements fresh basil wonderfully.
This versatile dip can also be used as a sauce or a spread, in sandwiches or on bagels.

2 tsp	olive or vegetable oil	10 mL
2	large onions, sliced (4 cups/1 L)	2
1 tbsp	balsamic vinegar	15 mL
1-1/2 tsp	granulated sugar	7 mL
1 cup	light (5%) sour cream	250 mL
1/2 cup	2% plain yogurt	125 mL
1/4 cup	chopped fresh basil*	50 mL
1/4 tsp	each salt and pepper	1 mL

1 In nonstick skillet, heat oil over medium-high heat. Stir in onions and cook, stirring, for 5 minutes. Stir in vinegar and 1 tsp (5 mL) of the sugar. Reduce heat to low; cook, covered but stirring occasionally, for 20 to 30 minutes or until well caramelized and deep golden. Let cool completely.

2 Coarsely chop cooked onions; place in bowl. Stir in sour cream, yogurt, basil, salt, pepper and remaining sugar. Add more salt to taste. Cover and refrigerate for 30 minutes before serving. *Makes about 2-1/2 cups (625 mL).*

Make ahead: Cover and refrigerate for up to 2 days.

Note about Salt

The amount of sodium in the salt you add to taste is not included in the mg of sodium in the recipe's nutrition information. If you add 1/2 tsp (2 mL) of salt, you will add 1300 mg of sodium to the total recipe. To determine the amount per serving, divide the total sodium added by the number of servings.

*Substitution Tip

Instead of fresh basil, you can use 1/4 cup (50 mL) chopped fresh parsley plus 1 tsp (5 mL) dried basil.

Homemade Tortilla Chips

You can make you own crisp, flavorful, lower-fat tortilla chips. Cut soft flour tortillas into wedges; spread in single layer on baking sheet and bake in 375°F (190°C) oven for 3 to 5 minutes or until crisp.

For seasoned chips, before baking, brush very lightly with beaten egg white and sprinkle with dried or chopped fresh oregano or rosemary or with a combination of herbs, or with sesame seeds, poppy seeds or freshly grated Parmesan cheese.

Per 2 tbsp (25 mL):

calories	35
protein	2 g
total fat	1 g
cholesterol	2 mg
carbohydrate	5 g
sodium	44 mg

R.D.I. Vit A 1%, E 1%, C 2%, Folate 2%, Ca 4%(41 mg), Iron 1%, Zinc 1%.

Canada's Food Guide Serving:
¼ 🥕

Creamy Crab Dip

I find that frozen crabmeat has more flavor and a better texture than canned. Imitation crab is also fine. Of course, fresh Canadian crab is a hands-down winner to be used as a special treat. In summer, use chopped fresh chives instead of the parsley. This makes a tasty dip for vegetables, sliced French bread or low-fat chips such as baked tortilla chips (or Homemade Tortilla Chips on page 13).

1-1/2 cups	frozen crabmeat, thawed and thoroughly drained (7 oz/200 g)	375 mL
1 cup	light (5%) sour cream	250 mL
1/2 cup	2% plain yogurt	125 mL
1/2 cup	finely chopped celery	125 mL
2 tbsp	chopped fresh parsley and/or fresh dill	25 mL
1 tbsp	prepared horseradish	15 mL
1/2 tsp	Dijon mustard	2 mL
1/4 tsp	each salt, pepper and hot pepper sauce	1 mL

▌ In small bowl, combine crab, sour cream, yogurt, celery, parsley, horseradish, mustard, salt, pepper and hot pepper sauce; mix well. Cover and refrigerate for 1 hour. *Makes 2-1/2 cups (625 mL).*

Make ahead: Cover and refrigerate for up to 2 days.

Per 2 tbsp (25 mL):

calories	24
protein	2 g
total fat	1 g
saturated fat	trace
cholesterol	5 mg
carbohydrate	2 g
dietary fiber	0 g
sodium	103 mg

R.D.I. Vit A 1%, C 2%, Folate 1%, Ca 4%(40 mg), Iron 2%, Zinc 1%.

Black Bean Dip with Veggie Topping

This dip is a favorite with all my children. When Susie makes it, she cooks the onions and spices in the microwave (see sidebar). My sons sometimes omit the cooking and just mix everything in a food processor. Serve with baked tortilla chips or vegetables.

1 tsp	vegetable oil	5 mL
1/4 cup	chopped onion	50 mL
1	large clove garlic, minced	1
1	sweet green pepper, chopped	1
1/2 tsp	each ground coriander, ground cumin and chili powder	2 mL
1/4 tsp	cayenne pepper or crushed red pepper flakes	1 mL
1	can (19 oz/540 mL) black beans, drained and rinsed	1
2 tbsp	fresh lime or lemon juice	25 mL
3 tbsp	chopped packed fresh coriander (cilantro)	50 mL
1	small tomato, chopped	1

1 In large nonstick skillet, heat oil over medium heat; cook onion, garlic and half of the green pepper until onion is tender, about 5 minutes, stirring occasionally. Add ground coriander, cumin, chili powder and cayenne; cook, stirring, for 30 seconds. Remove from heat.

2 In food processor, process beans and lime juice. Add onion mixture and half of the fresh coriander; process until smooth. If too thick, add up to 1/4 cup (50 mL) water, 1 tbsp (15 mL) at a time, processing until smooth. Cover and refrigerate for at least 1 hour or for up to 3 days.

3 Spoon into serving dish. Sprinkle with remaining green pepper, coriander and tomato. *Makes 2 cups (500 mL).*

Make ahead: Through step 2, refrigerate for up to 3 days.

Pinto Bean Dip

Substitute 1 can (19 oz/540 mL) pinto beans, drained and rinsed, for the black beans. If using pinto beans, it may not be necessary to add water.

Microwave Method

In microwaveable dish, combine oil, onion, garlic, half of the green pepper, ground coriander, cumin, chili powder and cayenne. Cover with plastic wrap, slightly vented; microwave on High for 2 minutes. Continue recipe at step 2 of Black Bean Dip.

Per 2 tbsp (25 mL):

calories	39
protein	2 g
total fat	trace
cholesterol	0 mg
carbohydrate	7 g
dietary fiber	2 g
sodium	57 mg

R.D.I. Vit A 1%, E 1%, C 12%, Folate 17%, Ca 1% (10 mg), Iron 4%, Zinc 3%.

Canada's Food Guide Serving:
¼ ▶

Herbed Yogurt-Cheese

I keep this versatile yogurt-cheese in the refrigerator and use it as a topping for baked potatoes, as a spread in pita sandwiches or to mix with a little light mayonnaise when making tuna or chicken sandwiches. Don't overdo the garlic because it becomes much stronger in flavor after a few days.

Herbed Light Cream Cheese

Substitute 1 cup (250 mL), or 8 oz (250 g), light, tub or 17% cream cheese for the drained yogurt, or mix the light cream cheese with 1/2 tsp (2 mL) each herbs de Provence and grated lemon rind.

2 cups	2% plain yogurt (Balkan-style or no gelatin) or 1 cup (250 mL) extra-thick yogurt	500 mL
2 tbsp	chopped green onions or chives	25 mL
2 tbsp	finely chopped fresh parsley	25 mL
1 tbsp	finely chopped fresh dill and/or basil	15 mL
Half to 1	clove garlic, minced	Half to 1
1/4 to 1/2 tsp	each salt and pepper	1 to 2 mL

1 Place plain yogurt in cheesecloth-lined sieve set over bowl or in yogurt drainer; refrigerate for 3 hours or overnight or until reduced to 1 cup (250 mL).

2 In bowl, combine drained yogurt, onions, parsley, dill, garlic, salt and pepper, mixing well. Cover and refrigerate for at least 4 hours. *Makes 1 cup (250 mL).*

Make ahead: Cover and refrigerate for up to 3 days.

Per 2 tbsp (25 mL):

calories	29
protein	3 g
total fat	1 g
saturated fat	trace
cholesterol	2 mg
carbohydrate	3 g
sodium	99 mg

R.D.I. Vit A 1%, C 3%, Folate 4%, Ca 9% (97 mg), Iron 1%, Zinc 5%.

Canada's Food Guide Serving: 1/4

Mushroom Bruschetta

Pile any kind or combination of mushrooms — shiitake, portobello, oyster — on this tasty bruschetta. Serve as a starter at brunch, as a snack or cut into smaller pieces for hors d'oeuvres.

1	piece (6-inch/15 cm) baguette or Italian loaf	1
1	clove garlic, halved	1
1 tbsp	butter	15 mL
6 cups	sliced mushrooms (1 lb/500 g)	1.5 L
1/4 cup	chopped green onions	50 mL
1/4 cup	chopped fresh basil or 2 tsp (10 mL) dried	50 mL
1/4 cup	coarsely chopped fresh parsley	50 mL
1/2 cup	freshly grated Parmesan cheese	125 mL

1 Slice bread crosswise into 1/2-inch (1 cm) thick diagonal slices. Place on baking sheet; broil, turning once, for 2 minutes or until golden. Rub tops with cut side of garlic; discard garlic.

2 In large nonstick skillet, melt butter over medium-high heat. Add mushrooms; cook, shaking pan and stirring often, for about 8 minutes or until mushrooms are browned and liquid is evaporated. Stir in onions, basil and parsley; cook for 1 minute.

3 Spoon mixture over garlic side of bread; sprinkle with cheese.

4 Broil for about 3 minutes or until cheese melts. Serve hot or warm. *Makes 12 pieces.*

Make ahead: Through step 2, cover and refrigerate for up to 1 day. Through step 3 up to 1 hour ahead.

Tomato Basil Bruschetta

In bowl, toss together 2 large tomatoes, diced, 1/4 cup (50 mL) chopped fresh basil (lightly packed), 1 clove garlic, finely chopped, and salt and pepper to taste; let stand for 15 minutes. Prepare bread with garlic as directed. Brush lightly with olive oil and top with tomato mixture.

Per piece:

calories	57
protein	3 g
total fat	3 g
saturated fat	1 g
cholesterol	6 mg
carbohydrate	6 g
dietary fiber	1 g
sodium	136 mg

R.D.I. Vit A 2%, E 1%, C 3%, Folate 4%, Ca 6% (69 mg), Iron 6%, Zinc 5%.

Canada's Food Guide Serving:
¼ 🌾 ½ 🥕

Marinated Mussels

Tantalizing tastes make these a winning hors d'oeuvre. They are also perfect for a first course at a dinner party or as part of an antipasto platter.

2 lb	mussels (45 to 50)	1 kg
Half	each small yellow and red sweet pepper, diced	Half
1/4 cup	chopped fresh coriander (cilantro)	50 mL
1/4 cup	minced green onions	50 mL
2 tbsp	fresh lime or lemon juice	25 mL
2 tbsp	soy sauce	25 mL
1 tbsp	roasted sesame oil	15 mL
1 tbsp	minced gingerroot	15 mL
1/2 tsp	hot chili paste or hot pepper sauce	2 mL

1 Wash mussels and remove any hairy beards; discard any mussels that have broken or open shells or don't close when tapped.

2 Place in large heavy saucepan; add 1/2 cup (125 mL) water. Cover and cook over medium-high heat until mussels open, about 5 minutes; drain and let cool. Discard any mussels that do not open.

3 Meanwhile, in large bowl, stir together sweet peppers, coriander, onions, lime juice, soy sauce, sesame oil, ginger and hot chili paste.

4 Remove mussels from shells, reserving shells. Add mussels to bowl; cover and marinate for at least 30 minutes.

5 Arrange half the mussel shells on large platter; fill each with mussel and some marinade. *Makes about 45 pieces or 6 first-course servings.*

Make ahead: Through step 4, cover and refrigerate for up to 6 hours.

Per piece:
calories 12
protein 1 g
total fat 1 g
   cholesterol 2 mg
carbohydrate 1 g
sodium 38 mg
R.D.I. Vit A 1%, C 7%, Folate 1%, Ca 0%(2 mg), Iron 2%, Zinc 1%.

Garlic Green Beans with Flavored Oil

When I visited Wendy Bowle-Evans, at her home in the tiny village of Regusse in the Provence area of France, she made this with flavorful walnut oil and the skinny green beans you find everywhere in France. In the center of the platter, she heaped marinated wild mushrooms, which her husband, Jean-Jacques Virgros, had picked.

To Serve Hot

Drain cooked beans but do not cool. Add hot beans in step 3, garnish and serve immediately.

1-1/2 lb	green beans	750 g
1	clove garlic, chopped	1
1 tsp	salt	5 mL
1 tbsp	balsamic or red wine vinegar	15 mL
1 tbsp	walnut or sesame oil	15 mL
Garnish:		
1	tomato, cut in wedges, or 1/4 cup (50 mL) thinly sliced red cabbage	1

1 Remove stem ends from green beans. In large pot of boiling water, cook beans for 4 to 5 minutes or until tender; drain and cool under cold water. Drain well.

2 On serving platter and using pestle or back of fork, crush garlic with salt to form paste: stir in vinegar then oil.

3 Add green beans; stir to coat in garlic mixture. Let stand for 15 minutes.

4 Garnish with tomato or red cabbage. *Makes 8 servings.*

Make ahead: Through step 1, wrap in paper towels then place in plastic bag and refrigerate for up to 1 day. Through step 2 for up to 2 hours.

Per serving:

calories	46
protein	2 g
total fat	2 g
saturated fat	trace
cholesterol	0 mg
carbohydrate	7 g
dietary fiber	2 g
sodium	290 mg

R.D.I. Vit A 6%, E 2%, C 17%, Folate 12%, Ca 3% (35 mg), Iron 7%, Zinc 3%.

Canada's Food Guide Serving:
1½

Fresh Beet and Onion Salad

This simple yet tasty Spanish salad goes well with almost any meat, fish or poultry.
Be sure to use extra-virgin olive oil and coarsely ground black pepper.

4	medium beets (1 lb/500 g)	4
2 tbsp	red wine vinegar	25 mL
1 tbsp	extra-virgin olive oil	15 mL
1/4 tsp	each granulated sugar, salt and coarsely ground pepper	1 mL
	Lettuce leaves or watercress (optional)	
1 cup	thinly sliced Spanish onion	250 mL

1 Trim beets, leaving 1 inch (2.5 cm) of stems. In pot of boiling water, cook beets, covered, until tender when tested with fork, about 40 minutes. Drain and let cool; slip off skins. Cut into 1/4-inch (5 mm) thick slices.

2 Combine vinegar, oil, sugar, salt and pepper.

3 Line shallow serving dish with lettuce (if using). Arrange half of the beets on dish; top with half of the onion. Drizzle with half of the dressing. Repeat layers. Let stand for 30 minutes. *Makes 4 servings.*

Make ahead: Through step 2, cover and refrigerate for up to 6 hours. Through step 3, set aside for 30 minutes.

Serving Tip

Slice, dice or coarsely grate cold cooked beets then drizzle with balsamic vinegar or toss with Herb and Ginger Vinaigrette (page 57)

Cooking Tip

See page 140 for more information on beets.

Nutrition Tip

Beets are high in folate, potassium and fiber. Beet greens are very high in beta carotene (vitamin A) and potassium and are a source of vitamin C and folate.

Per serving:

calories	85
protein	2 g
total fat	4 g
cholesterol	0 mg
carbohydrate	13 g
dietary fiber	2 g
sodium	211 mg

R.D.I. Vit E 7%, C 10%, Folate 35%, Ca 2% (23 mg), Iron 6%, Zinc 4%.

Canada's Food Guide Serving:

1½

Yogurt Parsley Dressing

This delicious, creamy, all-purpose dressing goes well in almost any salad, such as seafood, potato, cooked vegetable or just plain leafy greens. The parsley is essential — it adds a fresh flavor — but I like to add other fresh herbs as well.

1 cup	**1% or 2% plain yogurt**	250 mL
1/2 cup	**light mayonnaise**	125 mL
1/2 cup	**chopped fresh parsley**	125 mL
2 tbsp	**fresh lemon juice**	25 mL
1	**small clove garlic, minced**	1
1 tsp	**each Dijon mustard and salt**	5 mL
1/4 tsp	**pepper**	1 mL

I In small bowl, stir together yogurt, mayonnaise, parsley, lemon juice, garlic, mustard, salt and pepper. Cover and refrigerate. *Makes 1-2/3 cups (400 mL).*

Make-ahead: Cover and refrigerate for up to 1 week.

Buttermilk Dill Dressing: Substitute buttermilk for yogurt; add 1/3 cup (75 mL) (or more to taste) chopped fresh dill or 1 tsp (5 mL) dried dillweed.

Basil Yogurt Dressing: Add 1/3 cup (75 mL) chopped fresh basil.

Tarragon Yogurt Dressing: Add 1/4 cup (50 mL) chopped fresh tarragon or 2 tsp (10 mL) dried.

Creamy Caesar Yogurt Dressing: Add another clove garlic, minced, and 1/4 cup (50 mL) freshly grated Parmesan cheese.

Per 1 tbsp (15 mL):

calories	20
protein	1 g
total fat	1 g
cholesterol	0 mg
carbohydrate	1 g
sodium	125 mg

R.D.I. Vit A 1%, C 3%, Folate 1%, Ca 2% (18 mg), Iron 1%, Zinc 1%.

Herb and Ginger Vinaigrette

*You'll love this combination of herbs, ginger and garlic tossed with a mixture
of fresh greens or drizzled over a plate of thickly sliced tomatoes. If fresh coriander
(cilantro) and basil aren't available, substitute 1/4 cup (50 mL) chopped fresh
parsley and a pinch each of crushed dried basil and coriander leaves.*

2 tbsp	balsamic or rice vinegar	25 mL
1 tbsp	each soy sauce, fresh lemon juice and olive oil	15 mL
2 tsp	granulated sugar	10 mL
1 tsp	minced gingerroot	5 mL
1	clove garlic, minced	1
2 tbsp	each chopped fresh basil and coriander (cilantro)	25 mL

I In small bowl, whisk together vinegar, soy sauce, lemon juice, oil, sugar, ginger and
garlic. Stir in basil and coriander. Season with salt and pepper to taste.
Makes about 1/2 cup (125 mL), enough for green salad to serve 8.

Tomato, Arugula and Red Onion Salad: In salad bowl or on platter, toss
4 medium tomatoes, cut in wedges, 1 bunch arugula and a few paper-thin slices of
red onion separated into rings with enough of this vinaigrette to moisten.
Makes 4 servings.

Substituting Dried Herbs For Fresh

As a rough guideline, substitute
one-third the amount of dried
herb for the amount of fresh
herb. For example, in a recipe
calling for 1 tbsp (15 mL) fresh
rosemary, use 1 tsp (5 mL)
dried. For the mild herbs, such as
parsley, dill and basil, because I
use large amounts of the fresh,
I use less than one-third of the
dried, usually about 1 tsp (5 mL).
Dried coriander seeds should not
be substituted for the fresh. In
some cases you can use a bit of
the dried leaves.

Add fresh herbs toward or at
the end of the cooking time or
just before serving. Dried herbs
are usually added near the
beginning of the cooking time.

Per 1 tbsp (15 mL):

calories	26
protein	0 g
total fat	2 g
saturated fat	trace
cholesterol	0 mg
carbohydrate	3 g
sodium	130 mg

R.D.I. Vit E 2%, C 2%, Ca 0% (3 mg),
Iron 1%.

Asian Carrot and Mushroom Noodle Soup

Light and fresh tasting yet with the heartiness of pasta and chicken, this soup can be a main course or appetizer. For variety, use other kinds of noodles and substitute spinach or chopped bok choy for the snow peas.

*Substitution Tip

Substitute rice stick noodles or rice vermicelli for the egg noodles; add them with the coriander and simmer for 2 minutes or until noodles are tender.

1 tsp	vegetable oil	5 mL
2	cloves garlic, minced	2
1 tbsp	minced gingerroot	15 mL
3	green onions, chopped	3
1/8 tsp	red pepper flakes	0.5 mL
1 cup	thickly sliced mushrooms	250 mL
3/4 cup	thinly sliced carrots	175 mL
2 cups	each chicken stock and water	500 mL
1 tbsp	fresh lime or lemon juice	15 mL
2 tsp	each fish sauce, sodium-reduced soy sauce and sesame oil	10 mL
2 oz	fine egg noodles (approx. 3/4 cup/175 mL)*	60 g
6 oz	boneless skinless chicken breast (about 1), cut in thin strips	175 g
3/4 cup	trimmed halved snow peas	175 mL
3 tbsp	chopped fresh coriander (cilantro)	50 mL

Per serving:

calories	135
protein	13 g
total fat	4 g
saturated fat	1 g
cholesterol	31 mg
carbohydrate	13 g
dietary fiber	2 g
sodium	596 mg

R.D.I. Vit A 43%, E 3%, C 13%, Folate 9%, Ca 3% (31 mg), Iron 9%, Zinc 11%.

Canada's Food Guide Serving:
¼ 🌾 ¾ 🥕 ¼ 🍗

1 In saucepan, heat oil over medium heat; cook garlic, ginger, onions and red pepper flakes, stirring, for 2 minutes.

2 Add mushrooms and carrots; cook, stirring, for about 5 minutes or until moisture is evaporated.

3 Add stock, water, lime juice, fish sauce, soy sauce and sesame oil; bring to boil. Reduce heat and simmer, uncovered, for 10 minutes.

4 Stir in noodles and chicken; bring to boil. Reduce heat and simmer for 5 minutes. Add snow peas; cook for 2 minutes. Stir in coriander.
Makes 5 servings, about 1 cup (250 mL) each.

Make ahead: Cover and refrigerate for up to 1 day.

Spicy Thai Chicken Noodle Soup

Liven up an old favorite by adding Thai seasonings. I think you'll like the freshness of lime juice and rind. Use rice stick vermicelli noodles, available at many supermarkets. To measure, first break into about 3-inch (8 cm) pieces. If you prefer an even spicier soup, add more hot chili paste to taste before serving.

1 tsp	vegetable oil	5 mL
3	cloves garlic, minced	3
1 tbsp	ground cumin	15 mL
1/2 tsp	turmeric	2 mL
8 oz	boneless skinless chicken breasts, thinly sliced	250 g
5 cups	chicken stock	1.25 L
2 tsp	each minced gingerroot and granulated sugar	10 mL
1 tsp	hot chili paste	5 mL
1/2 tsp	grated lime rind	2 mL
2 tbsp	fresh lime juice	25 mL
2 cups	broken rice stick vermicelli (3-1/2 oz/100 g)	500 mL
1 cup	each bean sprouts and coarsely chopped romaine lettuce	250 mL
2 tbsp	chopped fresh coriander (cilantro)	25 mL

1 In saucepan, heat oil over medium heat; cook garlic, cumin and turmeric, stirring constantly, for 1 minute.

2 Add chicken, chicken stock, ginger, sugar, chili paste, lime rind and juice; bring to boil. Reduce heat and simmer for 5 minutes.

3 Add rice stick vermicelli; simmer for 3 minutes. Add bean sprouts and lettuce; cook for 1 minute. Ladle into bowls; sprinkle with coriander.
Makes 6 servings, about 1-1/4 cups (300 mL) each.

Make ahead: Through step 2, cover and refrigerate for up to 1 day.

Per serving:

calories	163
protein	15 g
total fat	3 g
saturated fat	1 g
cholesterol	22 mg
carbohydrate	18 g
dietary fiber	1 g
sodium	677 mg

R.D.I. Vit A 4%, E 3%, C 10%, Folate 12%, Ca 3% (36 mg), Iron 13%, Zinc 10%.

Canada's Food Guide Serving:
¼ 🌾 ½ 🥕 ½ 🌶

Chinese Shrimp and Scallop Soup

This meal-in-a-pot is really a soup with unlimited possibilities. Smaller servings make a wonderful first course as well. Use raw shrimp if possible — because they are more flavorful.

1 oz	dried Chinese or shiitake mushrooms (about 1 cup/250 mL)	30 g
4 oz	rice stick vermicelli or fine egg noodles, broken (about 1-3/4 cups/425 mL)	125 g
1 tbsp	sesame oil	15 mL
3	green onions (including tops), chopped	3
2	large cloves garlic, minced	2
1 tbsp	grated gingerroot	15 mL
3-1/2 cups	each chicken stock and water	875 mL
1/4 cup	rice wine vinegar	50 mL
1 tbsp	soy sauce	15 mL
1 tsp	granulated sugar	5 mL
1/4 tsp	hot pepper sauce or hot chili paste	1 mL
4 cups	coarsely chopped bok choy (leaves and stalks)	1 L
8 oz	large shrimp, peeled and deveined	250 g
8 oz	sea scallops, halved horizontally	250 g

Cooking Tips

For a heartier soup, add 1/2 cup (125 mL) thickly sliced bamboo shoots or celery along with the stock.

For a spicier soup, add more hot pepper sauce to taste. Garnish with chopped fresh coriander (cilantro).

1 In small bowl, cover mushrooms with hot water; let stand for 20 minutes. Drain. Discard tough stems; thinly slice caps. Set aside. Meanwhile, if using rice stick vermicelli, cover with hot water; let soak for 20 minutes. Drain and set aside.

2 In large saucepan, heat 1 tsp (5 mL) of the oil over medium heat; cook onions, garlic and ginger, stirring, for 2 minutes. Stir in mushrooms. Pour in stock, water, vinegar, soy sauce, remaining 2 tsp (10 mL) oil, sugar and hot pepper sauce, bring to boil. Reduce heat to low and simmer, uncovered, for 15 minutes.

3 Stir in egg noodles if using; cook, uncovered, for 4 to 5 minutes. Stir in bok choy, shrimp and scallops; simmer for 2 minutes or until shrimp turn pink and bok choy wilts. Stir in rice stick noodles if using.

Makes 8 servings, about 1 cup (250 mL) each.

Make ahead: Through step 2, cover and refrigerate for up to 1 day.

Per serving:

calories	152
protein	13 g
total fat	3 g
saturated fat	1 g
cholesterol	42 mg
carbohydrate	17 g
dietary fiber	1 g
sodium	566 mg

R.D.I. Vit A 11%, E 2%, C 18%, Folate 13%, Ca 6% (64 mg), Iron 10%, Zinc 12%.

Canada's Food Guide Serving:
¼ 〰 ½ 🌱 ½ 🍗

Thai Coconut, Ginger and Chicken Soup
(Gai Tom Ka)

Everyone loves this unique and flavorful soup. Next to Pad Thai, it's the most popular menu item in Thai restaurants. For this Canadian version, I've used grated lime rind for kaffir lime leaves, grated lemon rind for lemongrass and fresh gingerroot for galangal. However, I don't recommend using soy sauce instead of fish sauce. This version is quite hot. For a milder soup, use less red pepper flakes.

1-2/3 cups	light unsweetened coconut milk (1 can/398 mL)	400 mL
1 cup	chicken stock	250 mL
	Grated rind from 1 medium lime OR 2 kaffir leaves, torn into pieces, discarding stem	
	Grated rind from half medium lemon OR 1 stalk lemongrass, lower 1/3 only, sliced diagonally into 1-inch/2 cm pieces	
1 tbsp	minced gingerroot	15 mL
1/4 tsp	red pepper flakes OR ground fresh chili paste OR 1 small hot red pepper, chopped	1 mL
4 oz	boneless skinless chicken breasts, thinly sliced and cut in 1-inch (2.5 cm) lengths	125 g
1 cup	straw, oyster or regular mushrooms, sliced or halved	250 mL
Quarter	sweet red pepper, cut in thin strips	Quarter
2 tbsp	fish sauce	25 mL
1/4 cup	chopped fresh coriander (cilantro)	50 mL
1 tbsp	fresh lime juice, or to taste	15 mL

1 In saucepan over medium heat, simmer (don't boil) coconut milk, stock, lime and lemon rinds, ginger and red pepper flakes for 5 minutes.

2 Add chicken, mushrooms and red pepper; cook, stirring often, until chicken is no longer pink inside, about 5 minutes. Stir in fish sauce, coriander and lime juice to taste. *Makes 4 servings, about 3/4 cup (175 mL) each.*

Per serving:
calories	**119**
protein	**9 g**
total fat	**6 g**
saturated fat	5 g
cholesterol	17 mg
carbohydrate	**8 g**
sodium	**627 mg**

R.D.I. Vit A 8%, E 1%, C 42%, Folate 4%, Ca 1% (12 mg), Iron 3%, Zinc 4%.

Canada's Food Guide Serving:
¼ 🥕 ¼ 🍗

Porcini Mushroom Bisque

I absolutely love the rich, woodsy flavor of porcini mushrooms and sometimes double the amount in this recipe. This very elegant dinner party starter can be a clear soup or a cream soup, puréed in a food processor or left chunky.

3/4 cup	dried porcini mushrooms	175 mL
1/2 cup	boiling water	125 mL
1 tsp	olive oil	5 mL
1	small onion, finely chopped	1
Pinch	dried thyme	Pinch
1 lb	fresh mushrooms, coarsely chopped (about 5 cups/1.25 L)	500 g
2 tbsp	all-purpose flour	25 mL
2 cups	vegetable or chicken stock	500 mL
2 cups	2% milk	500 mL
1/4 cup	chopped fresh parsley or green onions (including tops)	50 mL

1 Rinse dried porcini mushrooms under cold water to remove grit. Place in small bowl and pour in boiling water; let stand for 30 minutes. Drain, reserving liquid; chop mushrooms and set aside.

2 In heavy or nonstick saucepan, heat oil over medium heat; cook onion and thyme for 3 minutes. Add fresh and porcini mushrooms; cook, stirring often, for 5 minutes. Sprinkle with flour and stir until mixed; cook, stirring, for 1 minute. Add stock and reserved porcini mushroom liquid; bring to boil. Reduce heat, cover and simmer for 20 minutes.

3 In food processor or blender, purée half of the mixture. Return to saucepan and stir until blended. Stir in milk; heat over medium heat, stirring, until hot.

4 Add salt and pepper to taste. Ladle into bowls; sprinkle with parsley.
Makes 6 servings, about 3/4 cup (175 mL) each.

Make ahead: Through step 3, cover and refrigerate for up to 2 days.

Mushroom Soup

Follow recipe for Porcini Mushroom Bisque but omit the porcini mushrooms and soaking liquid. Add bay leaf along with stock; discard before puréeing.

Lactose Intolerant?

Follow recipe for Porcini Mushroom Bisque but replace milk with more stock.

Per serving:	
calories	85
protein	5 g
total fat	3 g
saturated fat	1 g
cholesterol	6 mg
carbohydrate	11 g
dietary fiber	2 g
sodium	258 mg

R.D.I. Vit A 5%, D 17%, E 2%, C 10%, Folate 9%, Ca 10% (110 mg), Iron 9%, Zinc 11%.

Canada's Food Guide Serving:

1 🥕 ¼ 🥛

73

Eating Well As We Get Older

As we age it gets harder to meet our nutrition needs, and healthy eating becomes even more important. In addition to the gradual declines in gastrointestinal function, muscle mass and immunity, most of us face some additional stress and disability such as arthritis, high blood pressure, elevated cholesterol levels or diabetes. What's more, medications more commonly used later in life, such as diuretics, laxatives, heart and cancer drugs, may promote nutrient losses or affect our appetites.

HEALTHY EATING TIPS: Older People

- Follow the same basic principles of healthy eating (page 1). Keep your diet low in fat and increase your intake of complex carbohydrates and fiber by eating more vegetables, fruit, whole grains and legumes (dried beans, peas and lentils).
- Make every food choice count nutritionally. As your metabolism slows down, your need for calories drops but your need for nutrients doesn't. You may need even more of some nutrients since the gastrointestinal tract doesn't absorb nutrients as well as it once did.
- Vegetables, fruits, legumes (dried beans, peas and lentils) and whole grains take on an even greater significance — not just for the complex carbohydrate and fiber but as the main source of antioxidant vitamins and minerals. Antioxidant nutrients fight against heart disease and cancer and keep the immune system in top form.
- Pay close attention to your intake of calcium and vitamin D, particularly if you don't get outdoors. (See pages 94 and 97.)
- Make sure you drink lots of fluids. Declining kidney function and a poor thirst response can put you at risk of dehydration. Dehydration is linked to mental confusion.
- Lastly, consider a multivitamin supplement if your food intake is low or restricted for any reason. A multivitamin doesn't make up for a faulty diet but it can help you meet your needs for certain nutrients like calcium and vitamin D.

Lentil, Barley and Sweet Potato Soup

I freeze some of this thick, comforting, yet light winter soup for those times when there is no time to cook. The fresh dill and parsley make this soup special. It is better to omit them than to use dried. If the soup seems too thick after cooking the potato, add more stock.

1/2 cup	dried green lentils	125 mL
2 tsp	vegetable oil	10 mL
2	cloves garlic, minced	2
2	carrots, coarsely chopped (about 1 cup/250 mL)	2
2	stalks celery, chopped	2
1	medium onion, chopped	1
1-1/2 tsp	dried thyme	7 mL
1/3 cup	pearl or pot barley	75 mL
6 cups	chicken or vegetable stock	1.5 L
2	bay leaves	2
1	sweet potato (12 oz/375 g), peeled and diced (2 cups/500 mL)	1
1/4 cup	each chopped fresh dill and parsley	50 mL

1 Rinse lentils, discarding any blemished or shrivelled ones; set aside.

2 In large saucepan, heat oil over medium heat; cook garlic, carrots, celery, onion and thyme, stirring often, for about 5 minutes or until softened.

3 Stir in lentils and barley; pour in stock. Add bay leaves; bring to boil. Reduce heat and simmer, covered, for 50 minutes.

4 Stir in sweet potato; cover and simmer for 20 minutes or until barley and potato are tender. Discard bay leaves.

5 Stir in dill and parsley. Season with salt and pepper to taste.
Makes 8 servings, about 1 cup (250 mL) each.

Make ahead: Through step 4, cover and refrigerate for up to 2 days or freeze for up to 1 month. After 4 hours, soup thickens (because barley absorbs the liquid); add 2 cups (500 mL) more stock and reheat.

Lentil, Barley, Sweet Potato and Fennel Soup
Substitute 3 cups (750 mL) chopped fresh fennel for the carrots and celery. It's delicious!

Lentils
Lentils are an excellent source of fiber, the B-vitamin folate and vegetable protein. Unlike most dried beans, they do not require any soaking, making them not only more convenient, but also an ideal addition to soups and stews.

To use canned lentils, add 1 can (19 oz/540 mL), drained, during last 10 minutes of cooking.

Per serving:

calories	161
protein	9 g
total fat	3 g
saturated fat	0 g
cholesterol	0 mg
carbohydrate	26 g
dietary fiber	4 g
sodium	611 mg

R.D.I. Vit A 103%, E 8%, C 18%, Folate 38%, Ca 4% (43 mg), Iron 18%, Zinc 12%.

Canada's Food Guide Serving:
¼ 🌾 1 🥕 ¼ 🍠

Mulligatawny Soup

British ingredients teamed with Indian spicing
make this a popular soup in India. Serve this simplified Canadian
version when you have leftover chicken or turkey.

2 tsp	vegetable oil	10 mL
4	cloves garlic, minced	4
4 tsp	minced gingerroot or 2 tsp (10 mL) ground ginger	20 mL
1 to 2 tsp	curry powder or curry paste	5 to 10 mL
1/2 tsp	cinnamon	2 mL
1	potato, peeled and chopped	1
1	apple, peeled and chopped	1
3 cups	turkey or chicken stock	750 mL
2 cups	fresh or frozen chopped mixed vegetables	500 mL
2 cups	diced cooked chicken or turkey	500 mL
1/2 tsp	salt	2 mL
2 tbsp	chopped fresh coriander (cilantro) or parsley	25 mL

1 In large nonstick saucepan, heat oil over medium heat; cook garlic, ginger, curry powder and cinnamon, stirring, for 1 minute.

2 Add potato, apple, stock and mixed vegetables; cover and simmer for 20 minutes or until vegetables are tender.

3 In food processor or blender, purée vegetable mixture until smooth; return to saucepan. Add chicken and salt; heat through.

4 Ladle into bowls; sprinkle with coriander. *Makes 6 servings, about 1 cup (250 mL) each.*

Make ahead: Through step 3, cover and refrigerate for up to 1 day.

Per serving:
calories 192
protein 18 g
total fat 6 g
saturated fat 1 g
cholesterol 42 mg
carbohydrate 17 g
dietary fiber 3 g
sodium 642 mg
R.D.I. Vit A 25%, E 7%, C 8%,
Folate 8%, Ca 3% (37 mg), Iron 11%,
Zinc 17%.

Canada's Food Guide Serving:

1 🥕 ¾ 🍗

Quick Black Bean, Corn and Tomato Soup

I developed this recipe for my children to cook at university.
It's homemade soup from a can — and it's a great fast and nutritious supper.
You can substitute red kidney beans for the black beans.

2 tsp	olive oil	10 mL
2	onions, chopped	2
4 tsp	chili powder	20 mL
1	can (28 oz/796 mL) stewed tomatoes	1
1-3/4 cups	vegetable or chicken stock	425 mL
1	can (19 oz/540 mL) black beans, drained and rinsed	1
1-1/2 cups	corn kernels	375 mL
2 tbsp	coarsely chopped packed fresh coriander (cilantro)	25 mL

1 In large heavy saucepan, heat oil over medium heat; cook onions and chili powder, stirring often, for 5 to 8 minutes or until tender.

2 Coarsely chop tomatoes; add to onions along with stock, black beans and corn. Simmer, stirring often, for 5 to 10 minutes or until slightly thickened. Stir in coriander. *Makes 6 servings, about 1-1/3 cups (325 mL) each.*

Make ahead: Cover and refrigerate for up to 3 days.

Nutrition Tip

Black beans are very high in the B-vitamin folate, fiber and iron. They also contain some calcium.

Student's Supper Menu

Grilled Cheese Sandwich on Whole Wheat (or Cheese and Crackers)
Quick Black Bean, Corn and Tomato Soup (this page)
Raw Carrots
Orange

Per serving:

calories	187
protein	9 g
total fat	3 g
saturated fat	trace
cholesterol	0 mg
carbohydrate	36 g
dietary fiber	7 g
sodium	715 mg

R.D.I. Vit A 14%, E 8%, C 37%, Folate 52%, Ca 7% (78 mg), Iron 20%, Zinc 14%.

Canada's Food Guide Serving:
2 🥕 ½ 🫑

Onion and Potato Soup

*I made this thick soup one night when my shelves were
almost bare except for a large Spanish onion, some potatoes and Parmesan cheese.
The second time I made it, I added cabbage for an extra flavor dimension.
Serve with toast or sprinkle croutons onto each bowl.*

1 tbsp	olive oil	15 mL
1	large Spanish onion, coarsely chopped (2-1/2 cups/625 mL)	1
2	medium-large potatoes, peeled and diced (2-1/2 cups/625 mL)	2
1	can (10 oz/284 mL) chicken or vegetable broth	1
4 cups	water	1 L
3 cups	thinly sliced cabbage	750 mL
1 tsp	each salt and granulated sugar	5 mL
1/2 tsp	pepper	2 mL
1/2 cup	freshly grated Parmesan cheese	125 mL

1 In large heavy saucepan, heat oil over medium-low heat; cook onion, covered and stirring occasionally, for 10 to 15 minutes or until very tender.

2 Add potatoes; cook, uncovered and stirring frequently, for 2 minutes. Add broth and water; bring to boil. Cover, reduce heat and simmer for 10 to 15 minutes or until potatoes are tender.

3 Add cabbage; cover and simmer for 5 minutes or until cabbage is tender. Stir in salt, sugar and pepper.

4 Ladle into bowls; sprinkle with Parmesan. *Makes 8 servings, 1 cup (250 mL) each.*

Make ahead: Through step 3, cover and refrigerate for up to 3 days or freeze for up to 1 month. (Potatoes become mushy with freezing; purée soup or stir well.)

Per serving:

calories	**110**
protein	**6 g**
total fat	**4 g**
saturated fat	**2 g**
cholesterol	**5 mg**
carbohydrate	**13 g**
dietary fiber	**2 g**
sodium	**648 mg**

R.D.I. Vit A 1%, E 3%, C 17%, Folate 7%, Ca 10% (111 mg), Iron 4%, Zinc 6%.

Canada's Food Guide Serving:
1

78

Gazpacho

My daughter, Susie, learned this recipe at a restaurant in Spain where she once worked. She was told to add the vinegar just before serving. I added the tomato juice and reduced the amount of olive oil. It's the perfect soup for a hot summer's day. I also make this soup when I'm trying to lose a few pounds — it's filling and satisfying, full of good nutrients yet low in calories. I have it with toast, which I rub with a cut clove of garlic then cut into croutons.

2	cloves garlic	2
Half	onion, quartered	Half
1	sweet green or red pepper, seeded and quartered	1
4	tomatoes, quartered	4
1	cucumber (10-inch/25 cm) peeled, quartered and seeded	1
2 cups	tomato juice or 1 can (19 oz/540 mL) tomatoes, puréed	500 mL
1/4 cup	lightly packed coarsely chopped fresh basil or coriander (cilantro) or parsley or dill	50 mL
1/4 cup	balsamic or red wine vinegar*	50 mL
2 tbsp	extra-virgin olive oil	25 mL
1/2 tsp	each salt, pepper and hot pepper sauce	2 mL
1 cup	vegetable or chicken stock or water (optional)	250 mL

1 In food processor or blender, with machine running, drop garlic into feed tube, then onion; turn machine off. Add green pepper, tomatoes and cucumber; process until finely chopped. Transfer to large bowl.

2 Add tomato juice, basil, vinegar, oil, salt, pepper and hot pepper sauce. Add stock if mixture is too thick. Cover and refrigerate for 30 minutes. Serve cold.
Makes 8 servings, about 1 cup (250 mL) each.

Make ahead: Cover and refrigerate for up to 2 days.

* Substitution Tip

Vinegars vary in strength and flavor. You can substitute one kind for another in many recipes, but the amount you use might vary. To be on the safe side when substituting, add half the amount called for in a recipe, taste, then add more if desired.

Per serving:

calories	74
protein	2 g
total fat	4 g
saturated fat	1 g
cholesterol	0 mg
carbohydrate	10 g
dietary fiber	2 g
sodium	365 mg

R.D.I. Vit A 9%, E 13%, C 53%, Folate 14%, Ca 2% (20 mg), Iron 6%, Zinc 3%.

Canada's Food Guide Serving:
2 🥕

Pasta

Pasta with Chick-Peas and Spinach

Easy Creamy Turkey Fettuccine

Summer Corn and Tomato Pasta

Fettuccine with Pesto

Linguine with Shrimp and Fresh Basil

Pad Thai

Penne with Tomato, Tuna and Lemon

Thai Noodle and Vegetable Stir-Fry

Singapore-Style Noodles

Chinese Noodle and Shrimp Party Platter

Wild Mushroom and Spinach Lasagna

Grilled Italian Sausage and Red Peppers with Penne

Vegetable Tortellini Casserole with Cheese Topping

Penne with Sweet Red Peppers, Black Olives and Arugula

Skillet Pork Curry with Apples and Chinese Noodles

Lemon, Dill and Parsley Orzo

Beef, Tomato and Mushroom Rigatoni

Spicy Chicken with Broccoli and Chinese Noodles

Two-Cheese Pasta and Tomatoes

Nutrition Notes

Restaurant Food: "Dining Out in Good Health"

Calcium: "Bone Up with These Facts on Calcium"

Vitamin D: "Vitamin D: How To Get It"

Nutrition for Athletes: "Going for Gold with Healthy Eating"

Pasta with Chick-Peas and Spinach

This simple pasta dish is so delicious that you'll want to make it often.
Serve as a main course or side dish.

4 oz	medium pasta shells (1-2/3 cups/400 mL)	125 g
1	pkg (10 oz/284 g) fresh spinach, stemmed and coarsely chopped	1
1	can (19 oz/540 mL) chick-peas, drained and rinsed	1
1	clove garlic, chopped	1
1/2 cup	vegetable or chicken stock or water	125 mL
1 tsp	anchovy paste (optional)	5 mL
1/4 tsp	each salt and pepper	1 mL
	Grated rind or zest of half a medium lemon	

1 In large pot of boiling water, cook pasta until tender but firm. Add spinach and return to boil; drain.

2 Meanwhile, in food processor, purée half of the chick-peas with the garlic, stock, and anchovy paste (if using) until smooth; stir into drained pasta. Stir in remaining chick-peas, salt, pepper and lemon rind. *Makes 3 servings.*

Per serving:

calories	331
protein	16 g
total fat	3 g
saturated fat	trace
cholesterol	0 mg
carbohydrate	61 g
dietary fiber	8 g
sodium	634 mg

R.D.I. Vit A 68%, E 8%, C 22%, Folate 86%, Ca 14% (154 mg), Iron 34%, Zinc 24%.

Canada's Food Guide Serving:

1¼ 1½ 2

PASTA PRIMER

- Most pasta is made with fine semolina flour, which is made by grinding durum wheat and removing the bran and germ, leaving behind the endosperm. Because most of the vitamins and minerals are in the bran and the germ, the semolina flour may be enriched by adding niacin, thiamine, riboflavin, folate and iron. For a nutritional boost, buy pasta with added protein and fiber.
- To increase your fiber intake, choose pasta made from whole wheat flour, which includes the bran, germ and endosperm.
- For flavor and nutrients without a lot of extra fat, toss cooked pasta with cooked vegetables and a small amount of meat or fish or lower-fat cheese instead of cream, butter and regular cheese.

Easy Creamy Turkey Fettuccine

(handwritten: Tuna or) *(handwritten: ✓)*

Here's a great way to use up leftover turkey, chicken or ham after the holidays.
Evaporated 2 % milk has a cream-like thickness that works well in pasta dishes.

8 oz	fettuccine or spaghetti	250 g
2 tsp	olive oil	10 mL
2 cups	sliced mushrooms *or peppers (red/yellow/orange)*	500 mL
1 cup	each chopped red onion and sliced celery	250 mL
3	cloves garlic, minced	3
1-1/2 cups	cooked turkey strips* *(1 tin tuna = 1 c)*	375 mL
1 cup	2% evaporated milk	250 mL
1/4 cup	chopped fresh parsley *or cilantro*	50 mL
1/4 cup	packed chopped fresh basil** *(or 2 tsp dried w. onion)*	50 mL
1/4 cup	freshly grated Parmesan cheese	50 mL

1 In large pot of boiling water, cook fettuccine until tender but firm; drain.

2 Meanwhile, in large saucepan, heat oil over medium heat; cook mushrooms, onion, celery and garlic, stirring often, for 8 to 10 minutes or until tender.

3 Stir in turkey, milk, parsley, basil, cheese and hot pasta; simmer, stirring gently, for 3 minutes. Add salt and pepper to taste. *Makes 3 servings.*

Substitution Tips

* Instead of turkey, use cooked chicken, ham or shrimp or 1 can (6-1/2 oz/184 g) tuna or salmon.

** If fresh basil isn't available, substitute 2 tsp (10 mL) dried basil and cook it along with the onions.

Nutrition Tip

Evaporated milk has twice as much calcium as fresh milk.

LOWER-FAT PASTA SAUCES

- At home: Use a minimum of oil, butter and cream. Instead, use milk or evaporated skim milk, or ricotta cheese (whirl in blender or food processor for a creamy texture). Toss in ingredients such as garlic and hot peppers; they offer lots of flavor but little fat. Using strong cheeses such as Parmesan, allows you to use less.

- In stores: When purchasing a ready-made pasta sauce, check the ingredient list. If the first items are oil, butter, cream or cheese, it will be high in fat.

- In restaurants: If you are unsure about ingredients in a dish, ask your server. Go for dishes with lots of fresh vegetables and herbs.

Per serving:	
calories	584
protein	42 g
total fat	12 g
saturated fat	4 g
cholesterol	66 mg
carbohydrate	75 g
dietary fiber	5 g
sodium	338 mg

R.D.I. Vit A 10%, D 31%, E 11%,
C 30%, Folate 24%, Ca 39% (424 mg),
Iron 27%, Zinc 53%.

Canada's Food Guide Serving:
2¾ 2 ¾ 1¼

Summer Corn and Tomato Pasta

This pasta makes a great main course or side dish for a casual summer dinner.
It also packs well for lunch or picnics. Any kind of cooked beans can be used, but black
beans look most attractive. Or for a change, substitute shrimp or tuna for the beans.

2 cups	cooked fresh or frozen corn kernels	500 mL
5	medium tomatoes, cut in chunks (5 cups/1.25 L)	5
1 cup	cooked or canned black beans, drained and rinsed	250 mL
1/2 cup	finely chopped fresh coriander (cilantro) or basil	125 mL
1 tbsp	extra-virgin olive oil	15 mL
1	jalapeño pepper, seeded and minced, or 2 cloves garlic, minced	1
4	green onions, finely chopped	4
1 tsp	each salt and pepper	5 mL
8 oz	penne (3 cups/750 mL) or other short pasta	250 g
1 cup	crumbled feta cheese (5 oz/150 g)	250 mL

1 In large bowl, stir together corn, tomatoes, beans, coriander, oil, jalapeño pepper, green onions, salt and pepper; let stand at room temperature for 15 minutes or for up to 2 hours.

2 In large pot of boiling water, cook pasta for 8 minutes or until tender but firm; drain and return to pot.

3 Add tomato mixture; stir over medium heat just until heated through. Serve sprinkled with feta. *Makes 6 main-course or 10 side servings.*

Make ahead: To serve cold, rinse hot pasta under cold water and add to tomato mixture; cover and refrigerate for up to 1 day.

Per side serving:

calories	**210**
protein	**8 g**
total fat	**6 g**
saturated fat	3 g
cholesterol	13 mg
carbohydrate	**34 g**
dietary fiber	**4 g**
sodium	**448 mg**

R.D.I. Vit A 9%, E 6%, C 38%,
Folate 30%, Ca 9% (94 mg), Iron 11%,
Zinc 13%.

Canada's Food Guide Serving:
¾ 🌾 1 🥕 ¼ 🥛

Fettuccini with Pesto

The most heavenly and, without a doubt, the very best pesto that I ever tasted was in the Cinque Terre on the Ligurian coast in Italy. I think they used a small-leafed basil, which when coupled with the bright sun, salty Mediterranean breezes, hillside soil and the local cheeses produced an unbelievably wonderful, fragrant dish. Prepared pesto sauce is easily available at most stores; however, I've yet to taste one as good as homemade pesto made with fresh basil. The ideal pesto isn't oozing with oil, yet has a full flavor and is moist enough when mixed with cooked pasta. For this light version, I add some white bread to stabilize the sauce and to allow water to be added for moisture.

12 oz	fettuccine or spaghetti	375 g
Pesto Sauce:		
3	cloves garlic	3
1-1/2 cups	packed fresh basil	375 mL
2	slices white bread, crusts removed	2
2 tbsp	olive oil	25 mL
2 tbsp	pine nuts (optional)	25 mL
1/2 tsp	salt	2 mL
1/4 cup	freshly grated Parmesan cheese	50 mL

1 In large pot of boiling water, cook pasta for 8 to 10 minutes or until tender but firm; drain, reserving about 1/2 cup (125 mL) cooking water. Transfer pasta to serving bowl.

2 Pesto Sauce: Meanwhile, with food processor on, drop garlic through tube and process until chopped. Add basil, bread, oil, pine nuts (if using) and salt; process until well mixed, scraping down sides once or twice. Add 1/2 cup (125 mL) of the reserved cooking liquid (or hot water); process until blended. Stir in cheese.

3 Spoon over hot pasta; toss to mix, adding more cooking liquid if too dry. *Makes 4 servings.*

Make ahead: Through step 2 (pesto sauce), cover and refrigerate for up to 4 days.

Freezing Pesto

It's great to have homemade pesto on hand. Just freeze it in ice cube trays, then transfer to airtight container and freeze for up to 6 months.

Using Pesto

Add a large spoonful of pesto to soups or stews; spread on pizza instead of tomato sauce; stuff under the skin of chicken or use in the Pesto Salmon Fillets recipe on page 204.

Per serving:

calories	441
protein	15 g
total fat	11 g
saturated fat	2 g
cholesterol	5 mg
carbohydrate	71 g
dietary fiber	4 g
sodium	467 mg

R.D.I. Vit A 1%, E 9%, C 2%, Folate 14%, Ca 13% (143 mg), Iron 11%, Zinc 18%.

Canada's Food Guide Serving:
3½ 🌾 ¼ 🥕

Dining Out in Good Health

In the overall scheme of things the occasional meal out isn't going to break a healthy eating pattern. But if you eat in restaurants frequently, you run the risk of consuming more fat than is healthy.

HEALTHY EATING TIPS: Dining Out

- Make your needs known. Good restaurants will accommodate your requests to grill rather than fry an entrée, to serve lighter salad dressings, to serve sauces on the side, or to prepare a tomato-based pasta dish even if it isn't on the menu.
- Watch out for these typical downfalls: butter on the bread, high-fat appetizers like Caesar salads or cream soups, deep-fried entrées and rich desserts.
- Make trade-offs: if you have Caesar salad, go light on the rest of the meal; or choose a very light meal so that you can enjoy one of the special desserts.
- Lower-fat choices in fast food restaurants are sometimes hard to come by but these types of foods are better if available:
  - a grilled rather than a fried chicken sandwich
  - a plain hamburger with lettuce and tomatoes rather than a burger with double patties, cheese, bacon and sauce
  - a vegetarian pizza rather than one with pepperoni, bacon and extra cheese
  - low-fat milk or juice instead of a milkshake
  - low-fat salad dressings rather than regular ones
  - cereal or a low-fat muffin instead of an egg-cheese-bacon on buttered toast or croissant
  - submarines or sandwiches on whole wheat bread without the butter or mayonnaise
  - chili or bean-based dishes

Linguine with Shrimp and Fresh Basil

With shrimp in the freezer and canned tomatoes on the shelf, you can make this
any time of year. You can also use frozen and thawed cooked shrimp.
Serve with a crisp salad of tossed greens.

1	can (28 oz/796 mL) tomatoes	1
1	can (5-1/2 oz/156 mL) tomato paste	1
1/2 cup	packed chopped fresh basil or 1 tbsp (15 mL) dried	125 mL
4	cloves garlic, minced	4
1	onion, chopped	1
1 tbsp	chopped fresh oregano or 1 tsp (5 mL) dried	15 mL
1 lb	large shrimp, peeled and deveined	500 g
12 oz	linguine, fettuccine or spaghetti	375 g
1/4 cup	freshly grated Parmesan cheese	50 mL

1 In saucepan, mash tomatoes with juice. Add tomato paste, half of the fresh basil
(all if using dried), garlic, onion and oregano; bring to boil. Reduce heat and simmer,
stirring occasionally, for 20 minutes or until onion is tender and sauce is thickened
slightly.

2 Add shrimp; cover and cook for about 3 minutes or just until shrimp are pink
and firm.

3 Meanwhile, in large pot of boiling water, cook linguine for 8 to 10 minutes or until
tender but firm; drain well. Toss with tomato sauce and remaining basil. Serve
sprinkled with Parmesan cheese. *Makes 4 servings.*

Make ahead: Through step 1, cover and refrigerate for up to 1 day.

Per serving:

calories	**527**
protein	**35 g**
total fat	**6 g**
saturated fat	2 g
cholesterol	**134 mg**
carbohydrate	**85 g**
dietary fiber	**8 g**
sodium	**601 mg**

R.D.I. Vit A 27%, E 27%, C 70%,
Folate 21%, Ca 19% (208 mg), Iron 39%,
Zinc 33%.

Canada's Food Guide Serving:
3 🌾 3¼ 🥕 1 🍗

Pad Thai

In Thailand, this noodle dish is eaten at any time or in any place — from restaurants to street stalls. Each cook adds a personal touch. My version is lower in fat and uses easily available ingredients.

Substitution Tip

For a more authentic Thai dish, substitute 3 tbsp (50 mL) dried chopped shrimp for the fresh. Pickled white radish or salted cabbage (1/4 cup/50 mL) is often added. Tamarind paste or juice is used instead of vinegar.

8 oz	medium-wide rice noodles	250 g
3 tbsp	fish sauce	50 mL
2 tbsp	rice vinegar or cider vinegar	25 mL
2 tbsp	granulated sugar	25 mL
1 tbsp	vegetable oil	15 mL
2	eggs, lightly beaten	2
3	large cloves garlic, finely chopped	3
1/4 tsp	red pepper flakes	1 mL
8 oz	large shrimp, peeled and deveined	250 g
4 oz	tofu, sliced in thin strips (about 1 cup/250 mL)	125 g
3 cups	bean sprouts	750 mL
6	green onions, chopped	6
1/2 cup	coarsely chopped fresh coriander (cilantro)	125 mL
1/4 cup	chopped unsalted peanuts	50 mL
1	lime, cut in wedges	1

Per serving:

calories	459
protein	24 g
total fat	13 g
saturated fat	2 g
cholesterol	172 mg
carbohydrate	62 g
dietary fiber	3 g
sodium	680 mg

R.D.I. Vit A 9%, D 9%, E 16%, C 30%, Folate 45%, Ca 11% (117 mg), Iron 31%, Zinc 30%.

Canada's Food Guide Serving:
1½ 🌾 1¾ 🥕 1½ 🍗

1 Soak noodles in hot water for 20 minutes; drain. In small bowl, mix together fish sauce, rice vinegar and sugar; set aside.

2 In large nonstick wok or skillet, heat 1 tsp (5 mL) of the oil over medium-high heat; cook eggs, stirring, until scrambled. Cut into strips; transfer to side dish.

3 Wipe out pan; add remaining oil. Stir-fry garlic, red pepper flakes and shrimp for 2 minutes. Add tofu; stir-fry for 1 minute or until shrimp are pink and opaque.

4 Add noodles and 1/2 cup (125 mL) water; cook, stirring, for 2 to 3 minutes or until noodles are tender. Stir in fish sauce mixture, bean sprouts and half of the onions; toss to mix well. Transfer to serving dish. Top with eggs, remaining onions, coriander and peanuts. Garnish with lime. *Makes 4 servings.*

Penne with Tomato, Tuna and Lemon

*Serve small portions of this dynamic, Italian-style pasta dish as
a first course or larger servings for a main course. Even when the fridge is bare,
you'll likely have these ingredients on hand.
The lemon rind adds a tremendous zing to the dish*

8 oz	penne, rotini or rigatoni pasta	250 g
1 tbsp	olive oil	15 mL
4	cloves garlic, minced (2 tsp/10 mL)	4
1 tsp	fennel seeds, crushed	5 mL
1/4 tsp	crushed red pepper flakes	1 mL
1	can (19 oz/540 mL) chopped tomatoes or 3 cups (750 mL) coarsely chopped fresh	1
1	can (6.5 oz/184 g) water-packed tuna, drained	1
2 tbsp	drained capers	25 mL
1/4 cup	coarsely chopped fresh flat-leaf parsley	50 mL
	Grated rind of half a lemon (1/2 tsp/2 mL)	

1 In large pot of boiling water, cook pasta for 8 to 10 minutes or until tender but firm; drain well.

2 Meanwhile, in large nonstick skillet, heat oil over medium heat; cook garlic, fennel seeds and red pepper flakes, stirring, until garlic is softened, about 2 minutes.

3 Stir in tomatoes, tuna and capers; bring to boil. Reduce heat and simmer for 8 to 10 minutes or until thickened slightly.

4 Stir in cooked pasta, parsley, lemon rind, and salt and pepper to taste.

Makes 3 main-course or 6 first-course servings.

Per main-course serving:

calories	425
protein	24 g
total fat	7 g
saturated fat	1 g
cholesterol	15 mg
carbohydrate	67 g
dietary fiber	6 g
sodium	561 mg

R.D.I. Vit A 15%, E 13%, C 43%, Folate 15%, Ca 8% (90 mg), Iron 24%, Zinc 21%.

Canada's Food Guide Serving:
2¾ 🌾 1½ 🥕 1 🌙

Thai Noodle and Vegetable Stir-Fry

This quick and easy stir-fry with spunky Thai flavors makes a great quick supper.
Add shrimp, scallops, chicken, meat or tofu for a heartier dish.
Consider broccoli, bok choy, cauliflower, carrots, mushrooms, celery, zucchini,
cabbage or green beans for the stir-fry vegetables.

4 oz	rice vermicelli noodles*	125 g
4 cups	chopped stir-fry vegetables or 1 pkg (500 g) frozen mixed Chinese vegetables, thawed	1 L
1 tbsp	vegetable oil	15 mL
2	cloves garlic, minced	2
1	fresh red chili pepper, seeded and chopped, or 1/4 tsp (1 mL) red pepper flakes	1
3 tbsp	oyster sauce	50 mL
2 tbsp	fresh lime or lemon juice	25 mL
1 tbsp	each fish sauce (or soy sauce) and minced gingerroot	15 mL
1 tsp	granulated sugar	5 mL
3	green onions, chopped	3
2 tbsp	toasted sesame seeds	25 mL

1 Soak noodles in hot water for 15 minutes; drain.

2 In large pot of boiling water, cook vegetables for 2 minutes. Add noodles; cook for 1 minute or until tender. Drain well.

3 Meanwhile, in wok or large nonstick skillet, heat oil over medium heat; stir-fry garlic for 1 minute. Stir in chili pepper, oyster sauce, lime juice, fish sauce, ginger and sugar; cook for 1 minute.

4 Mix noodle mixture into wok; cook, stirring, for 1 minute. Sprinkle with green onions and sesame seeds. *Makes 4 servings.*

* Substitution Tip

Instead of rice vermicelli noodles, cook 6 oz (175 g) spaghettini or other very thin noodle in saucepan of boiling water for 6 minutes. Add vegetables; bring to boil. Reduce heat and simmer for 2 to 4 minutes or until just tender; drain and continue with step 3.

Per serving:

calories	210
protein	8 g
total fat	7 g
saturated fat	1 mg
cholesterol	0 mg
carbohydrate	31 g
dietary fiber	4 g
sodium	995 mg

R.D.I. Vit A 78%, E 12%, C 60%, Folate 24%, Ca 6% (14 mg), Iron 14%, Zinc 14%.

Canada's Food Guide Serving:

1 🌾 2 🥕

Singapore-Style Noodles

Although it looks long, this vegetarian dish can be made in less than half an hour.

* Substitution Tip

If rice noodles are unavailable, substitute 6 oz (175 g) very thin noodles and cook for 8 to 10 minutes in large pot of boiling water.

Singapore-Style Noodles with Shrimp and Chicken

Omit egg and tofu. Instead, after step 2, add 6 oz (175 g) boneless, skinless chicken, cut in strips, and 8 oz (250 g) peeled, deveined medium-to-large shrimp; stir-fry for about 5 minutes or until chicken is no longer pink inside and shrimp is bright pink. Continue with step 3.

6 oz	rice vermicelli noodles*	175 g
2 tsp	vegetable oil	10 mL
2	eggs, lightly beaten	2
2	large cloves garlic, minced	2
1	onion, thinly sliced	1
1 tbsp	minced gingerroot	15 mL
2 tsp	each curry powder and granulated sugar	10 mL
3/4 tsp	each ground cumin and ground coriander	4 mL
1/2 tsp	pepper or hot chili sauce or hot pepper sauce	2 mL
3/4 cup	vegetable stock	175 mL
1	each sweet green and red pepper, cut in thin strips	1
6 oz	firm tofu, cubed	175 g
2 cups	bean sprouts (5 oz/150 g)	500 mL
1/2 cup	sliced green onions	125 mL
1/4 cup	coarsely chopped fresh basil and/or coriander (cilantro)	50 mL
1/4 cup	sodium-reduced soy sauce	50 mL
1 tbsp	fresh lime juice	15 mL

Per serving:

calories	352
protein	17 g
total fat	10 g
saturated fat	2 g
cholesterol	108 mg
carbohydrate	52 g
dietary fiber	3 g
sodium	762 mg

R.D.I. Vit A 19%, D 9%, E 8%, C 135%, Folate 34%, Ca 15% (163 mg), Iron 51%, Zinc 23%.

Canada's Food Guide Serving:
1 🌾 2¾ 🥕 ¾ 🍗

1 Soak noodles in hot water for 20 minutes; drain. Meanwhile, in large nonstick skillet or wok, heat 1 tsp (5 mL) of the oil over medium heat; cook egg, stirring, until scrambled and set. Remove to plate. Cut into strips and keep warm.

2 In same skillet, heat remaining oil over medium-high heat; stir-fry garlic, onion, ginger, curry powder, sugar, cumin, ground coriander, pepper and 2 tbsp (25 mL) of the stock for 2 minutes. Add sweet peppers, tofu and 2 tbsp (25 mL) more of the stock; stir-fry for 2 to 3 minutes or until peppers are slightly softened.

3 Add drained noodles, remaining stock, half of the bean sprouts, the green onions, half of the basil, the soy sauce and lime juice; stir-fry until well coated. Stir in egg strips. Serve garnished with remaining bean sprouts and basil. *Makes 4 servings.*

Chinese Noodle and Shrimp Party Platter

I served this at a summer buffet party for my daughter, Susie, and her student friends.
The menu included grilled flank steak, sliced tomatoes with fresh basil and chèvre
and Black Bean and Corn Salad (page 45). They all raved about this dish

1	pkg (375 g) thin egg noodles or precooked (steamed) Chinese noodles	1
2 cups	coarsely shredded carrots	500 mL
2 cups	julienned seeded peeled cucumbers (1-1/2-inch/4 cm strips)	500 mL
5 cups	bean sprouts (12 oz/375 g)	1.25 L
1/2 cup	chopped fresh coriander	125 mL
1/4 cup	chopped fresh mint	50 mL
1 lb	large cooked peeled shrimp	500 g
1/4 cup	chopped peanuts (optional)	50 mL
Dressing:		
1/2 cup	sodium-reduced soy sauce	125 mL
1/4 cup	rice vinegar	50 mL
1 tbsp	sake or rice wine or scotch	15 mL
2 tbsp	granulated sugar	25 mL
2 tbsp	dark roasted sesame oil	25 mL
1/4 tsp	hot chili paste or hot pepper sauce	1 mL

1 Cook noodles according to package directions until tender yet firm; drain and rinse with water until cold. Drain well and transfer to center of very large platter.

2 Dressing: In small bowl, mix together soy sauce, vinegar, sake, sugar, oil and hot chili paste until sugar dissolves. Pour half of the dressing over noodles and toss to mix.

3 Arrange carrots and cucumber around noodles. Place bean sprouts on top of noodles; sprinkle with coriander and mint. Top with shrimp, and peanuts (if using).

4 Just before serving, drizzle with remaining dressing and toss lightly.
Makes 10 servings (1-1/2 cups /375 mL each).

Make ahead: Through step 3, cover and refrigerate for up to 6 hours.

Per serving:

calories	281
protein	20 g
total fat	6 g
saturated fat	1 g
cholesterol	130 mg
carbohydrate	37 g
dietary fiber	4 g
sodium	761 mg

R.D.I. Vit A 67%, E 3%, C 20%, Folate 23%, Ca 4% (47 mg), Iron 20%, Zinc 18%.

Canada's Food Guide Serving:

1¼ 🌾 1½ 🥕 1 🦐

Bone Up with These Facts on Calcium

How Much Calcium Do You Need?

In 1997 higher recommendations for calcium intake were released. Meeting these higher levels is a challenge, particularly for women, many of whom get less than 700 mg daily.

1997 Daily Calcium Recommendations*

Ages 9 to 18	1300 mg
Ages 19 to 50	1000 mg
Age 50 plus	1200 mg

*These recommendations were made by a Calcium Review Committee of the Food and Nutrition Board of the U.S. National Academy of Science, which included Canadian representatives. Health Canada plans to consider these recommendations when updating Canadian Nutrient Recommendations in the future.

The recipes in this book include a variety of calcium-rich foods — milk, cheese, yogurt, beans and dark green vegetables — because many Canadians, particularly women, aren't getting enough calcium, a crucial component of life-long bone health. In Canada, one in four women and one in eight men are at risk of developing osteoporosis, a debilitating disease in which bones become thin and porous and fracture easily. And there's mounting evidence that calcium is important for healthy blood pressure as well.

The Best Sources of Calcium

Milk products are the best dietary sources of calcium not only because they contain large amounts of calcium but also because of the vitamin D found in milk. Vitamin D is closely linked to the proper absorption and utilization of calcium. (See page 97.)

Other foods contribute to calcium intake but few can deliver the calcium of milk products. The calcium in spinach, for instance, is of little benefit because spinach contains a lot of oxalate, a substance that binds with the calcium making it largely unavailable. The same goes for the calcium in beet greens, sweet potatoes and rhubarb. However, the calcium in other plant sources like broccoli, kale and bok choy is well absorbed. It is difficult to meet the new calcium recommendations unless you consume 2 to 3 servings of milk products daily.

Don't Do Dairy?

If you can't or choose not to eat or drink milk products, include as many servings of non-dairy sources of calcium as possible and consider taking a calcium supplement.

Calcium Supplement Guide

- Calcium pills are sold as calcium carbonate, calcium gluconate or calcium lactate. These pills contain varying amounts of pure or elemental calcium. Always buy according to elemental calcium content, not the weight of the whole pill.
- Take only what you think you need to top up your diet, probably not more than 500 to 1000 mg of elemental calcium daily.

- Extra calcium is best obtained from a separate calcium supplement, not a multi-vitamin preparation. Don't take two or three multi-vitamin tablets for extra calcium as you run the risk of getting too much of other nutrients such as vitamin D. While it's a good idea to include extra vitamin D when you take a separate calcium supplement, don't exceed 400 IU per day.
- Drink extra water to reduce risk of developing kidney stones and prevent excess calcium settling in soft tissues.
- Take supplements between meals to increase absorption and to avoid interference with iron absorption.
- Avoid taking calcium along with bulk-forming laxatives. They interfere with calcium absorption.

Top Food Choices for Calcium

Dairy Sources	mg calcium
• milk, 1 cup (250 mL)	300
• evaporated skim milk, 1 cup (250 mL)	746
• cheese, 1-1/2 oz (45 g)	325
• yogurt, 3/4 cup (175 mL) 1% to 2%, plain	300
• yogurt, 2% fruit-flavored, 3/4 cup (175 mL)	250
• processed cheese, 45 g or 2 thin slices	225
• cottage cheese, 2% MF, 1/2 cup (125 mL)	75

Non-Dairy Sources	mg calcium
• tofu set with calcium sulphate, 1/2 cup (125 mL)	110
• salmon with crushed bones, half 213 g can	225
• 8 small sardines, 3 oz (90 g)	165
• 7 large scallops, 3 oz (90 g)	30

Non-Dairy Sources (continued)	mg calcium
1/2 c (125 mL) cooked	
• bok choy	80
• kale	45
• green cabbage	26
• broccoli	38
• brussels sprouts	30
• cauliflower	17
• rutabaga	36
• almonds, 1/4 cup, (50 g)	95
• sesame seeds, 1/4 cup, (50 g)	50
• sunflower seeds, 1/4 cup, (50 g)	40
• baked beans, navy beans, 3/4 cup (175 mL)	100
• pinto beans, chick-peas, kidney beans, 3/4 cup (175 mL)	50

Grilled Italian Sausage and Red Peppers
with Penne

I came upon this winning flavor combination one Labour Day when using up what was left in our cottage refrigerator. Grilling the sausages and peppers adds extra flavor. However, you can also cook them in a skillet.

12 oz	hot Italian sausages	375 g
2	large sweet red peppers	2
1 tbsp	olive oil	15 mL
1 cup	chopped onion	250 mL
12 oz	penne	375 g
4	large cloves garlic, finely chopped	4
3	large tomatoes, chopped	3
1/2 cup	chopped fresh dill or basil*	125 mL
1/2 tsp	each salt and pepper	2 mL
1/3 cup	grated light (19%) old Cheddar-style or Parmesan cheese	75 mL

*Substitution Tip

Instead of fresh dill or basil, add 1 tsp (5 mL) dried basil with the garlic and 1/2 cup (125 mL) fresh parsley with the salt.

Lower-Fat Tip

The fat content of sausages varies considerably. An average was used in this recipe. Here 12 grams of fat in each serving is from the sausages. This can be reduced by half if you use leaner sausages.

1 Prick sausages all over. Quarter and seed peppers. Place peppers on greased grill over medium heat; close lid and cook for 5 minutes. Move peppers to upper rack if possible. Place sausages on grill; close lid and cook for 20 minutes or until sausages are no longer pink in center, turning peppers and sausages after 10 minutes. Slice sausages; cut peppers into chunks.

2 Meanwhile, in large nonstick skillet, heat oil over medium heat; cook onion for 10 to 15 minutes or until tender, stirring occasionally.

3 Meanwhile, in large pot of boiling water, cook penne until tender but firm; drain well.

4 Add garlic to onion; increase heat to high. Add tomatoes; cook, stirring occasionally, for about 2 minutes or until heated through. Add dill, red peppers, sausages, penne, salt and pepper; toss to mix. Serve sprinkled with cheese.

Makes 4 servings (3 cups/750 mL each).

Make ahead: Through step 2, cover and refrigerate for up to 4 hours.

Per serving:

calories	604
protein	29 g
total fat	19 g
saturated fat	6 g
cholesterol	42 mg
carbohydrate	80 g
dietary fiber	7 g
sodium	909 mg

R.D.I. Vit A 44%, E 6%, C 262%, Folate 21%, Ca 12% (136 mg), Iron 24%, Zinc 25%.

Canada's Food Guide Serving:

3 🌾 3 🥕 1 🍗

Vegetable Tortellini Casserole
with Cheese Topping

Consider this casserole when you want a quick dish that all ages will enjoy. It's perfect for entertaining families and is a good choice when you want a change from lasagna.

1 tbsp	olive oil	15 mL
2	cloves garlic, minced	2
1	each medium onion and carrot, chopped	1
1	each sweet green and red pepper, chopped	1
1 tsp	each dried basil and oregano	5 mL
1/4 tsp	each salt and pepper	1 mL
1	can (28 oz/796 mL) stewed tomatoes	1
1	can (5-1/2 oz/156 mL) tomato paste	1
1 cup	corn kernels	250 mL
1 lb	cheese-filled tortellini	500 g
1 cup	grated part-skim mozzarella cheese	250 mL
1/4 cup	freshly grated Parmesan cheese	50 mL
2 tbsp	chopped fresh parsley	25 mL

1 In large nonstick skillet, heat oil over medium heat; cook garlic, onion, carrot, sweet peppers, basil, oregano, salt and pepper, stirring, for 5 minutes or until softened.

2 Stir in tomatoes and tomato paste; bring to boil. Reduce heat and simmer, uncovered, for 15 to 20 minutes or until thickened. Stir in corn.

3 Meanwhile, in large pot of boiling water, cook tortellini for 8 to 10 minutes or according to package directions. Drain and add to tomato sauce; pour into 13- x 9-inch (3 L) shallow baking dish.

4 Toss together mozzarella, Parmesan and parsley; sprinkle over casserole. Bake, uncovered, in 400°F (200°C) oven for 15 minutes or until bubbling and golden. *Makes 6 servings.*

Make ahead: Through step 3, cover and refrigerate for up to 2 days; remove from refrigerator 45 minutes before baking.

Menu Suggestion
Serve with Spinach Salad (page 38) and/or Indonesian Coleslaw (page 43) or asparagus.

Freezing Instructions
Wrap and freeze the cooked casserole for up to 2 weeks. Thaw in the refrigerator for up to 48 hours.

Per serving:	
calories	**499**
protein	**25 g**
total fat	**14 g**
saturated fat	**6 g**
cholesterol	**75 mg**
carbohydrate	**72 g**
dietary fiber	**8 g**
sodium	**1085 mg**

R.D.I. Vit A 75%, E 26%, C 162%, Folate 24%, Ca 41% (453 mg), Iron 32%, Zinc 33%.

Canada's Food Guide Serving:
2½ 🌾 4 🥕 ¾ 🥛

Skillet Pork Curry with Apples and Chinese Noodles

I usually have a package of precooked, steamed (not fried) Chinese or chow mein noodles in my refrigerator because they cook in less than 3 minutes (not to mention the fact that my son John loves them!). They are available in the produce section of most supermarkets. Any other very thin egg or regular noodle also works well, as does pasta. You could even serve this over rice instead of the noodles. Choose Red Delicious or Northern Spy apples.

1-1/2 lb	pork tenderloin or boneless fast-fry chops	750 g
1 tbsp	vegetable oil	15 mL
1 tsp	each ground coriander, ground cumin and turmeric	5 mL
1/2 tsp	each salt and red pepper flakes	2 mL
1/2 tsp	fennel seeds, crushed	2 mL
1	large onion, sliced	1
2	cloves garlic, minced	2
1 tbsp	minced gingerroot	15 mL
2	red-skinned apples, cored and cubed	2
1 cup	chicken stock	250 mL
1 tbsp	all-purpose flour	15 mL
1 cup	1% or 2% plain yogurt	250 mL
1 tbsp	liquid honey	15 mL
1	pkg (350 g) precooked Chinese noodles	1
1/3 cup	chopped fresh coriander (cilantro) or parsley	75 mL
1/4 cup	each raisins and chopped peanuts	50 mL

Per serving:

calories	478
protein	39 g
total fat	11 g
saturated fat	2 g
cholesterol	105 mg
carbohydrate	56 g
dietary fiber	4 g
sodium	411 mg

R.D.I. Vit A 2%, E 13%, C 7%, Folate 14%, Ca 10% (115 mg), Iron 22%, Zinc 44%.

Canada's Food Guide Serving:

1½ 🌾   1 🥕   ¼ 🥛   2 🍖

1 Trim fat from pork; cut across the grain into 3/4-inch (2 cm) wide strips.

2 In nonstick skillet, heat 1 tsp (5 mL) of the oil over high heat; brown half of the pork. Transfer to plate. Repeat with another 1 tsp (5 mL) oil and remaining pork.

3 Reduce heat to medium-low. Add remaining oil, ground coriander, cumin, turmeric, salt, red pepper flakes and fennel seeds; cook, stirring, for 1 minute. Add onion, garlic and ginger; cook, stirring often, for 5 minutes.

4 Add apples; cook, stirring often, for 5 minutes or until onion is tender. Pour in stock and bring to boil; reduce heat and stir in pork. Cover and simmer for about 3 minutes or until pork is barely pink inside.

5 Sprinkle flour over yogurt; add honey and stir to mix well. Stir into pork mixture.

6 Meanwhile, in large pot of boiling water, cook noodles for 1 to 2 minutes or until tender; drain and add to pork mixture, tossing to mix. Transfer to large platter. Sprinkle with coriander, raisins and peanuts. *Makes 6 servings.*

Lemon, Dill and Parsley Orzo

*Tiny rice-shaped pasta adds novelty
to the meal and makes a great side dish for chicken and fish.*

1 cup	orzo pasta	250 mL
2 tbsp	each chopped fresh dill and parsley	25 mL
2 tbsp	chopped green onions	25 mL
1 tbsp	olive oil	15 mL
1/2 tsp	grated lemon rind	2 mL
1 tbsp	fresh lemon juice	15 mL

1 In large pot of boiling salted water, cook orzo for 8 to 10 minutes or until tender but firm; drain well.

2 Toss with dill, parsley, onions, oil, lemon rind and juice. Season with salt and pepper to taste. *Makes 4 servings.*

Make ahead: Best served immediately. For a make-ahead dish, use rice instead of orzo. Cook long-grain white rice for 20 minutes, brown rice for 40 minutes.

Wild and Basmati Rice with Lemon and Herbs
Substitute 1/2 cup (125 mL) each brown basmati rice or long-grain brown rice and wild rice for pasta. Cook wild and brown rice in large saucepan of boiling water for 35 to 40 minutes or until wild rice splays and brown is tender; drain well. Continue with step 2. *Make ahead:* Cover and refrigerate for up to 1 day.

Per serving:

calories	191
protein	5 g
total fat	4 g
saturated fat	1 g
cholesterol	0 mg
carbohydrate	32 g
dietary fiber	2 g
sodium	114 mg

R.D.I. Vit A 1%, E 4%, C 8%, Folate 6%, Ca 1% (14 mg), Iron 5%, Zinc 7%.

Canada's Food Guide Serving:
1 ½ 🌾

Going for Gold with Healthy Eating

Healthy eating can contribute to a child's success at sports, but sports nutrition is fraught with misinformation.

HEALTHY EATING TIPS: Sports Nutrition for Kids

- The pre-game or pre-event meal isn't what wins the game. It's what the athlete eats, day in and day out, all year round that makes the most difference. And what should this be? The same healthy eating pattern we all should be eating. (See page 1.)
- Sufficient protein is easily obtained through healthy eating; protein supplements are not needed except in a few specialized situations.
- Fluid is important for maintaining strength and stamina. Dehydration can debilitate an athlete quickly, especially in hot and humid conditions. Don't wait until a child is thirsty to provide fluid. The child should start sipping water at least 2 hours before an event. Have water available during and after the event too. The amount varies from child to child, but 4 to 8 glasses of extra water is a good guideline.
- Water is the best fluid to keep a person hydrated. Cold water is okay; it is absorbed more quickly, and contrary to myth, it does not cause cramps.
- Sports drinks are recommended in events lasting more than an hour.
- The main purpose of a pre-competition meal is to prevent the discomfort of hunger and to keep blood sugars from falling to a point where tiredness and poor concentration set in. Plan a small meal of easily digested foods, eaten at least 2 hours before an event. Since fat and protein slow down digestion, the meal should consist mostly of carbohydrate-rich foods such as bread, cereal, pasta, rice, vegetables and fruit.
- Tournaments present extra problems, especially if they are out of town and there are long waits between games or events. Resist the temptation to rely on higher-fat fast foods for meals and to nibble on typical ball park or arena snacks such as donuts, chips, chocolate bars and pop.

Beef, Tomato and Mushroom Rigatoni

*I updated my family's favorite beef and tomato spaghetti sauce by adding lots
of mushrooms, garlic and chopped fresh basil. For a vegetarian version, omit the beef
and add tofu, chick-peas or cooked beans. You could also add dried mushrooms,
sun-dried tomatoes and/or a sweet green pepper.*

1 lb	extra-lean ground beef	500 g
2	onions, chopped	2
6	cloves garlic, minced	6
1 lb	thickly sliced mushrooms (6 cups/1.5 L)	500 g
2 tsp	dried Italian herb seasoning or dried oregano	10 mL
1	can (5-1/2 oz/156 mL) tomato paste	1
1	can (28 oz/796 mL) tomatoes	1
1 tsp	granulated sugar	5 mL
1/2 cup	chopped fresh basil or 1 tsp (5 mL) dried	125 mL
1/4 cup	chopped fresh flat-leaf parsley	50 mL
1 tsp	each salt and pepper	5 mL
12 oz	rigatoni (6 cups/1.5 L)*	375 g
1	bag (10 oz/284 g) fresh spinach, chopped (optional)	1
1/3 cup	freshly grated Parmesan cheese	75 mL

1 In large nonstick skillet, brown beef over medium heat; pour off all fat. Stir in
onions, garlic, mushrooms and Italian seasoning; cook, stirring occasionally, until
onions are softened, about 8 minutes.

2 Stir in tomato paste, tomatoes (breaking up with back of spoon), sugar and half of
the basil (or dried if using); bring to boil. Reduce heat and simmer for 10 minutes.
Add water if too thick. Stir in remaining fresh basil, parsley, salt and pepper.

3 Meanwhile, in large pot of boiling water, cook rigatoni until tender but firm, 8 to
10 minutes. Add spinach (if using); cook for 1 minute. Drain well and toss with
sauce. Sprinkle each serving with Parmesan cheese. *Makes 6 servings.*

Make ahead: Refrigerate up to one day. Reheat, stirring in hot water if mixture is dry.

*Substitution Tip

Rigatoni, the fat tubular pasta,
works well in this recipe, but
any kind can be used.

Per serving:

calories	434
protein	28 g
total fat	9 g
saturated fat	3 g
cholesterol	44 mg
carbohydrate	62 g
dietary fiber	7 g
sodium	770 mg

R.D.I. Vit A 17%, E 19%, C 55%,
Folate 22%, Ca 15% (164 mg), Iron 37%,
Zinc 57%.

Canada's Food Guide Serving:
2   3½   ¾

Sweet Potato, Squash and Bulgur

*Thick but juicy, this vibrantly colored dish has a pleasant balance of textures
and seasonings. For a main course, top each serving with a
spoonful of yogurt, shredded cheese and fresh coriander. As a side dish, serve with
roasts or chicken or turkey. This casserole is a great buffet dish.*

*Substitution Tip

Instead of fresh tomatoes, you
can use 1 can (19 oz/540 mL)
chopped tomatoes, drained.

Nutrition Tip

Sweet potatoes and squash
are very high in beta
carotene, which the body
converts to vitamin A. Sweet
red peppers are very high in
vitamin C.

1/2 cup	bulgur	125 mL
1 tbsp	olive oil	15 mL
1	onion, sliced	1
2	cloves garlic, chopped	2
1 tsp	each cumin seeds, dried oregano and paprika	5 mL
3 cups	cubed peeled butternut or winter squash (10 oz/320 g)	750 mL
1-1/2 cups	cubed peeled sweet potato (8 oz/250 g)	375 mL
1	sweet red or green pepper, chopped	1
2 cups	chopped tomatoes*	500 mL
3/4 cup	vegetable or chicken stock	175 mL
2 tbsp	balsamic vinegar	25 mL

1 In bowl, cover bulgur with 2 cups (500 mL) hot water; let stand for 15 minutes. Drain.

2 Meanwhile, in large nonstick wok or pan, heat oil over medium-high heat; cook
onion and garlic, stirring often, for 5 minutes or until onion is softened. Add cumin
seeds, oregano and paprika; cook, stirring, for 2 minutes. Add squash, sweet potato
and red pepper; cook, stirring, for 2 minutes.

3 Add tomatoes and stock; bring to simmer. Cover and cook for 15 minutes or until
vegetables are tender-crisp.

4 Stir in bulgur; simmer for 5 minutes. Stir in vinegar; season with salt and pepper
to taste. *Makes 4 main-course or 8 side-dish servings.*

Make ahead: Cover and refrigerate for up to 1 day.

Per main-course serving:

calories	241
protein	6 g
total fat	4 g
saturated fat	1 g
cholesterol	0 mg
carbohydrate	49 g
dietary fiber	7 g
sodium	136 mg

R.D.I. Vit A 191%, E 5%, C 150%,
Folate 25%, Ca 8% (91 mg), Iron 21%,
Zinc 11%.

Canada's Food Guide Serving:
1 🌾 3½ 🥕

Mushroom Lentil Burgers

Fresh coriander and ground cumin enliven these quick-to-prepare burgers.
Serve with Skillet Sweet Potatoes (page 147) and Spinach with Tomatoes and Cumin (page 139).
Or treat them as a burger and serve in a bun with roasted vegetables and tzatziki
or with the traditional trimmings.

Mushroom Lentil Tortilla Wrap

Spoon unshaped Mushroom Lentil Burger mixture down center of 4 large soft flour tortillas. Cover with sliced tomato, diced avocado and shredded lettuce or spinach leaves. Fold one side, then ends over filling and roll up. *Makes 4 servings.*

Nutrition Tip

Lentils are very high in folate and fiber, and are a good source of protein.

Per serving:

calories	**207**
protein	**11 g**
total fat	**3 g**
saturated fat	**trace**
cholesterol	**0 mg**
carbohydrate	**35 g**
dietary fiber	**6 g**
sodium	**478 mg**

R.D.I. Vit A 63%, E 7%, C 8%, Folate 89%, Ca 6% (64 mg), Iron 34%, Zinc 19%.

Canada's Food Guide Serving:
¼ 🌾 1 🥕 1 🫛

2 tsp	vegetable oil	10 mL
2	cloves garlic, minced	2
1	onion, finely chopped (1 cup/250 mL)	1
1/2 tsp	each ground cumin and ground coriander	2 mL
1-1/2 cups	diced mushrooms (about 3 oz/90 g)	375 mL
1	can (19 oz/540 mL) lentils, drained and rinsed	1
1	carrot, grated (about 1 cup/250 mL)	1
1/3 cup	fine dry bread crumbs	75 mL
1/4 cup	chopped fresh coriander (cilantro)	50 mL
1/4 tsp	each salt and pepper	1 mL

1 In nonstick skillet, heat 1 tsp (5 mL) of the oil over medium heat; cook garlic, onion, cumin and ground coriander, stirring, for 2 minutes. Add mushrooms; cook, stirring, for about 8 minutes or until just golden. Let cool.

2 In food processor, coarsely mash lentils. Using pulsing motion, add mushroom mixture and carrot; transfer to bowl. Stir in bread crumbs, coriander, salt and pepper; pressing firmly, shape into 4 patties.

3 In nonstick skillet, heat remaining oil over medium heat; cook burgers for 4 minutes on each side or until heated through. *Makes 4 servings.*

Make ahead: Through step 2, wrap well and refrigerate for up to 2 days or freeze for up to 1 month. Thaw before proceeding.

Chick-Pea Burgers

Hot pickled peppers add zing to these burgers.
Tuck them into pita pockets or buns with yogurt, fresh coriander, lettuce and tomatoes.
Or serve the mixture wrapped in a soft tortilla as in the tortilla wraps.

2 tsp	vegetable oil	10 mL
3	green onions (including tops), chopped	3
2	cloves garlic, minced	2
1 tsp	each dried oregano and chili powder	5 mL
1 cup	diced sweet red or green pepper and/or 1/4 to 1/2 cup (50 to 125 mL) chopped pickled hot peppers	250 mL
Half	tomato, chopped	Half
1	can (19 oz/540 mL) chick-peas, drained and rinsed	1
1/3 cup	fine dry bread crumbs	75 mL
2 tbsp	chopped fresh coriander (cilantro) or parsley	25 mL

1 In nonstick skillet, heat 1 tsp (5 mL) of the oil over medium heat; cook onions, garlic, oregano and chili powder, stirring, for 2 minutes. Add red pepper and tomato; cook, stirring, for about 3 minutes or until pepper is tender and liquid is evaporated.

2 In food processor, mix pepper mixture with chick-peas; transfer to bowl. Stir in bread crumbs, parsley, and salt and pepper to taste until well combined; pressing firmly, shape into 4 burgers.

3 In nonstick skillet, heat remaining oil over medium heat; cook burgers for 4 minutes on each side or until heated through. *Makes 4 servings.*

Make ahead: Through step 2, wrap well and refrigerate for up to 3 days or freeze for up to 1 month. Thaw before proceeding

Chick-Pea, Tomato, Coriander Tortilla Wraps

Omit bread crumbs. Spoon unshaped Chick-Pea Burger mixture down center of 4 large soft flour tortillas. Top with diced tomato, drizzle of yogurt, chopped fresh coriander and shredded lettuce or spinach. Fold one side, then ends over filling and roll up. *Makes 4 servings.*

Per serving:

calories	199
protein	9 g
total fat	5 g
saturated fat	trace
cholesterol	0 mg
carbohydrate	32 g
dietary fiber	4 g
sodium	293 mg

R.D.I. Vit A 13%, E 6%, C 82%, Folate 27%, Ca 5% (60 mg), Iron 14%, Zinc 11%.

Canada's Food Guide Serving:

¼ 🌾 ¾ 🥕 1 🫘

(121)

Mexican Brown Rice with **Tomatoes and Corn**

*This is a handy dish to make ahead and keep in the refrigerator ready
for a quick supper. I often top it with grated cheese and chopped fresh coriander.
Brown rice is higher in fiber than white, but long-grain white rice works well.
Use Mexican-style tomatoes, if available.*

* **Substitution Tip**

Regular brown rice instead of
converted can be used in
Mexican Brown Rice, but
cook it with the tomatoes and
water for about 35 minutes.

1 tbsp	olive oil	15 mL
4	cloves garlic, minced	4
1	large onion, chopped (1-1/3 cups/325 mL)	1
1 tbsp	chili powder	15 mL
1-1/2 tsp	each ground cumin and dried oregano	7 mL
1-1/3 cups	long-grain converted brown rice*	325 mL
1	can (19 oz/540 mL) stewed tomatoes	1
1/4 tsp	hot pepper sauce	1 mL
1 cup	each frozen corn and peas	250 mL
1/2 tsp	each salt and pepper	2 mL

1 In saucepan, heat oil over medium heat; cook garlic and onion, stirring,
for 3 minutes or until softened. Stir in chili powder, cumin and oregano; cook for
1 minute. Stir in rice until well coated.

2 Stir in 1 cup (250 mL) water, tomatoes and hot pepper sauce; bring to boil, breaking
up tomatoes with back of spoon. Reduce heat to low; cover and simmer for
20 minutes. Stir in corn and peas; simmer, covered, for 5 to 10 minutes or until rice
and vegetables are tender. Stir in salt and pepper. *Makes 4 servings.*

Make ahead: Cover and refrigerate for up to 3 days; reheat gently.

Per serving:

calories	404
protein	11 g
total fat	6 g
saturated fat	1 g
cholesterol	0 mg
carbohydrate	81 g
dietary fiber	5 g
sodium	738 mg

R.D.I. Vit A 18%, E 11%, C 45%,
Folate 23%, Ca 10% (111 mg), Iron 27%,
Zinc 11%.

Canada's Food Guide Serving:
2 🌾 2½ 🥕

Mexican Brown Rice with Beans: Add 1 can (19 oz/540 mL) red kidney or
black beans, drained and rinsed, and 1/2 cup (125 mL) water when adding corn and
peas; simmer, covered, for about 10 minutes. *Makes 4 servings.*

Couscous with **Tomato and Basil**

Couscous is a great convenience food. It is fast to prepare and can be used in many ways.
I like to add chopped tomato for color, texture and juiciness without extra fat or calories.
Fresh mint instead of basil is also tasty in this dish. For a more substantial meal, add currants
or raisins and chick-peas, then top with toasted pine nuts or sunflower seeds.

2 tsp	vegetable or olive oil	10 mL
2	cloves garlic, minced	2
2 tsp	dried basil** or 1/2 cup (125 mL) chopped fresh	10 mL
1-1/4 cups	water or vegetable or chicken stock	300 mL
1 cup	couscous	250 mL
1 cup	finely chopped tomatoes*	250 mL
1/4 cup	chopped fresh parsley	50 mL
	Salt and pepper	

1 In nonstick saucepan, heat oil over medium heat; cook garlic for 2 minutes or
   until softened.

2 Add basil (if using dried) and water; bring to boil. Stir in couscous. Cover and remove
   from heat. Let stand for 5 minutes. Fluff with fork. Stir in tomatoes, basil (if using
   fresh), parsley, and salt and pepper to taste. *Makes 4 servings.*

Make ahead: Cover and refrigerate for up to 1 day.

Cooking Tips

* Couscous is truly versatile. Instead of tomatoes, try stirring in sautéed mushrooms, toasted almonds or peanuts, shredded arugula or fresh or roasted sweet peppers.

** If you are using dried basil and it has been around for a year or so, increase the amount to 1 tbsp (15 mL).

Cholesterol-Lowering Tip

Don't be taken in by labels that claim the food is cholesterol-free. Many cholesterol-free foods, such as oil, margarine, potato chips and shortening, are high in fat and should be used sparingly. Fat, particularly saturated and trans fat (partially hydrogenated fat), does more to raise blood cholesterol than does the cholesterol in food.

Per serving:

calories	205
protein	6 g
total fat	3 g
saturated fat	trace
cholesterol	0 mg
carbohydrate	39 g
dietary fiber	3 g
sodium	14 mg

R.D.I. Vit A 7%, E 5%, C 17%, Folate 14%, Ca 3% (30 mg), Iron 9%, Zinc 6%.

Canada's Food Guide Serving:

1½ ¼

Lentil and Vegetable Curry

Spicy Lentil and Vegetable Tortilla Wraps

For each serving, warm large flour tortilla on paper towel in microwave on High for 15 seconds. Spoon 2/3 cup (150 mL) lentil mixture down center; top with 1 tbsp (15 mL) plain yogurt and sprinkling of fresh coriander. Fold one side over filling, then ends and roll up.

Nutrition Tip

Lentils are very high in folate, fiber, and are a good source of vegetable protein. They also contain some calcium.

Per serving:

calories	206
protein	11 g
total fat	3 g
saturated fat	trace
cholesterol	0 mg
carbohydrate	37 g
dietary fiber	7 g
sodium	24 mg

R.D.I. Vit A 55%, E 15%, C 30%, Folate 87%, Ca 4% (44 mg), Iron 30%, Zinc 18%.

Canada's Food Guide Serving:
2 🥕 ¾ 🍞

132

Top this curry with yogurt and a sprinkle of fresh coriander and serve with a spinach salad and crusty bread. I particularly like the mild combination of spices here. However, you may prefer to increase the amount of hot pepper. You could substitute 1 tbsp (15 mL) curry powder or 2 tbsp (25 mL) curry paste for the spices.

1 tbsp	vegetable oil	15 mL
1	onion, chopped	1
2	cloves garlic, minced	2
1 tbsp	minced gingerroot	15 mL
1/2 tsp	each ground cumin, turmeric and coriander	2 mL
1/4 tsp	each cinnamon and hot pepper flakes	1 mL
2 cups	water or vegetable stock	500 mL
1 cup	green lentils	250 mL
1	large potato, peeled and cubed	1
1 cup	each chopped carrots and corn kernels	250 mL
2	tomatoes, coarsely chopped (2 cups/500 mL)	2
1/4 cup	chopped fresh parsley or coriander (cilantro)	50 mL

1 In large heavy or nonstick saucepan, heat oil over medium heat; cook onion and garlic, stirring often, for 5 minutes or until softened.

2 Stir in ginger, cumin, turmeric, coriander, cinnamon and hot pepper flakes; cook, stirring, for 1 minute. Add water and lentils; bring to boil. Cover, reduce heat and simmer for 25 minutes.

3 Add potato and carrots; cover and cook for 15 minutes or until lentils and vegetables are tender. Stir in corn and tomatoes; cover and cook for 5 minutes or until heated through. Stir in parsley, and salt and pepper to taste. *Makes 6 servings.*

Make ahead: Cover and refrigerate for up to 2 days or freeze for up to 1 month.

Barley and Black Bean Casserole

Not only is this healthy dish packed with vitamins and fiber,
it is also tasty and satisfying. Serve with Greek Marinated Leg of Lamb (page 195)
or with any grilled meats or fish. It's also perfect with tofu and
roasted or grilled vegetables.

1 tbsp	vegetable oil	15 mL
1	onion, chopped	1
3	large cloves garlic, minced	3
1 cup	pearl or pot barley	250 mL
3 cups	vegetable or chicken stock	750 mL
2 cups	corn kernels	500 mL
1	can (19 oz/540 mL) black beans, drained and rinsed	1
1/2 cup	chopped fresh parsley or basil	125 mL
2 tbsp	fresh lemon or lime juice	25 mL
1	tomato, diced	1

1 In casserole, heat oil over medium heat; cook onion and garlic for 5 minutes or until softened. Stir in barley; pour in stock. Cover and bake in 350°F (180°C) oven for 1 hour. Stir in corn and black beans.

2 Bake for 5 minutes longer or until heated through and barley is tender. Stir in parsley, lemon juice and tomato. *Makes 10 servings.*

Make ahead: Through step 1, cover and refrigerate for up to 1 day. Add 2 tbsp (25 mL) stock or water, reheat in microwave and continue.

For more Vegetarian Main Dishes see also Pasta, Soup, Salad and Brunch sections.

Barley

Barley does not require pre-soaking. Generally, pearl and pot barley can be used interchangeably, requiring about 1 hour of cooking.

- Do not confuse pearl or pot barley with whole hulled barley, which is brownish and more fibrous (generally found at health food stores). Although whole hulled barley is somewhat higher in nutrients, because only the outer husk has been removed (pearl barley has also had the bran removed), it needs to be soaked and is considerably tougher.

- Barley is a very high source of soluble fiber (the same kind as in oat bran), which may reduce blood cholesterol.

Per serving:

calories	171
protein	6 g
total fat	2 g
saturated fat	trace
cholesterol	0 mg
carbohydrate	34 g
dietary fiber	5 g
sodium	282 mg

R.D.I. Vit A 3%, E 4%, C 15%, Folate 37%, Ca 2% (26 mg), Iron 14%, Zinc 12%.

Canada's Food Guide Serving:
¾ 🌾 ½ 🥕 ¼ 🫘

133

Vegetable Side Dishes

Spanish-Style Asparagus

Roasted Asparagus with Parmesan

Asparagus with Shaved Parmesan

Make-Ahead Cumin-Spiced Broccoli

Spiced Cabbage and Spinach

Spinach with Tomatoes and Cumin

Beet Greens with Lemon and Almonds

Tomato Gratin

Tomatoes Provençal

New Potatoes with Mint Pesto

Sesame-Spiced Oven-Fried Potatoes

Herb Roasted Potatoes and Onions

Skillet Sweet Potatoes

Carrots Provençal

Two-Potato Scallop

Broccoli Carrot Stir-Fry

Carrot and Squash Purée with Citrus

Braised Fennel with Parmesan

Grilled Marinated Portobello Mushrooms

Roasted Eggplant Slices with Roasted Garlic Purée

Roasted Winter Vegetables

Nutrition Notes

Phytochemicals: "Phyto…What?"

Menopause: "Menopause on the Menu"

To Serve Cold

Cool cooked asparagus under cold water; blot dry. (Asparagus can be refrigerated for up to 1 day.) Pour vinegar mixture over asparagus, turning to coat; cover and marinate for 30 to 60 minutes. Serve at room temperature.

Per serving:

calories	**56**
protein	**2 g**
total fat	**4 g**
saturated fat	1 g
cholesterol	0 mg
carbohydrate	**5 g**
dietary fiber	**1 g**
sodium	**152 mg**

R.D.I. Vit A 5%, E 7%, C 15%, Folate 53%, Ca 2% (18 mg), Iron 5%, Zinc 4%.

Canada's Food Guide Serving:
1¼ 🥕

Nutrition Tip

Asparagus is an excellent source of folate, a B vitamin.

Per serving:

calories	**54**
protein	**3 g**
total fat	**3 g**
saturated fat	1 g
cholesterol	2 mg
carbohydrate	**4 g**
dietary fiber	**1 g**
sodium	**211 mg**

R.D.I. Vit A 5%, E 6%, C 15%, Folate 53%, Ca 5% (60 mg), Iron 5%, Zinc 5%.

Canada's Food Guide Serving:
1¼ 🥕

Spanish-Style Asparagus

The idea for this recipe came from editor Doug Pepper. Other tasty additions would include sesame oil and soy sauce, or grated lemon or orange rind.

1 lb	asparagus	500 g
1 tbsp	each olive oil and balsamic vinegar	15 mL
1	small clove garlic, minced	1
1/4 tsp	each paprika, granulated sugar, salt and pepper	1 mL

1 Snap off tough ends of asparagus. Cook in saucepan of boiling water for 5 minutes or steam until tender-crisp; drain well. Place in shallow serving dish.

2 Whisk together oil, vinegar, garlic, paprika, sugar, salt and pepper; pour over hot asparagus, turning to coat. *Makes 4 servings.*

Roasted Asparagus with Parmesan

This amazing way to cook asparagus is my husband's favorite. I prefer thick asparagus for roasting. However, very thin asparagus is also scrumptious. It may take a minute less.

1 lb	asparagus	500 g
2 tsp	olive oil	10 mL
1/4 tsp	each salt and pepper	1 mL
2 tbsp	freshly grated Parmesan cheese	25 mL

1 Arrange asparagus in single layer on baking sheet; drizzle with oil; turn to coat. Sprinkle with salt and pepper. Bake in 500°F (260°C) oven for 8 minutes or until tender and slightly charred in places.

2 Transfer to shallow serving dish; sprinkle with Parmesan. *Makes 4 servings.*

Asparagus with Shaved Parmesan

Buy a chunk of the best Parmesan (Parmigiano-Reggiano) and grate it yourself.

1 lb	asparagus	500 g
1 tbsp	balsamic vinegar	15 mL
1/4 cup	coarsely grated Parmesan cheese	50 mL

1 Snap off tough ends of asparagus. Cook in saucepan of boiling water for 5 minutes or steam until tender-crisp; drain well. Place in shallow serving dish.

2 Sprinkle with vinegar; turn to coat. Sprinkle with Parmesan. *Makes 4 servings.*

Per serving:

calories	**51**
protein	**5 g**
total fat	**2 g**
saturated fat	**1 g**
cholesterol	**5 mg**
carbohydrate	**5 g**
dietary fiber	**1 g**
sodium	**125 mg**

R.D.I. Vit A 5%, E 4%, C 15%, Folate 53%, Ca 9% (102 mg), Iron 4%, Zinc 6%.

Canada's Food Guide Serving:
1¼

Make-Ahead Cumin-Spiced Broccoli

My friend Sandra Lawrence gave me this recipe for cumin-spiced broccoli with ginger. Use tender peeled broccoli stalks and florets, or use only the florets and save the stalks for soup or coleslaw.

6 cups	broccoli chunks (1 lb/500 g)	1.5 L
4 tsp	butter or soft margarine	20 mL
1 tsp	cumin seeds or ground cumin	5 mL
1 tbsp	grated gingerroot	15 mL
1/3 cup	milk (2% or whole)	75 mL
1 tbsp	cornstarch	15 mL

1 In saucepan of boiling water, cover and cook broccoli until fork-tender, about 5 minutes; drain well. Pulse in food processor until finely chopped but not smooth.

2 Meanwhile, in nonstick skillet, melt butter over medium heat; cook cumin seeds for about 1 minute or until lightly browned. Stir in hot broccoli and ginger.

3 Whisk milk with cornstarch; pour into broccoli and cook, stirring, for 2 minutes. Season with salt and pepper to taste. *Makes 4 servings, about 2/3 cup (150 mL) each.*

Make ahead: Cover and refrigerate for up to 2 hours or freeze for up to 2 weeks (cumin and ginger flavors strengthen with freezing).

Nutrition Tip

Broccoli is very high in vitamin C, beta carotene and folate.

Per serving:

calories	**81**
protein	**4 g**
total fat	**5 g**
saturated fat	**3 g**
cholesterol	**12 mg**
carbohydrate	**8 g**
dietary fiber	**2 g**
sodium	**74 mg**

R.D.I. Vit A 17%, D 4%, E 16%, C 110%, Folate 20%, Ca 7% (72 mg), Iron 9%, Zinc 5%.

Canada's Food Guide Serving:
2

Spiced Cabbage and Spinach

Nutrition Tip

Cabbage is a good source of vitamin C. Spinach is a good source of folate. Both contain fiber.

Vitamin C

Vitamin C is destroyed by prolonged cooking, and it also leaches into cooking liquid. To get the most vitamin C from vegetables, bring water to a boil before adding them and cook for a short time. Raw fruits and vegetables have the most vitamin C. Since vitamin C is water-soluble and is not stored by the body, you need to eat vitamin-C rich fruits and vegetables every day. If you take in too much, it is simply excreted.

Per serving:

calories	**74**
protein	**3 g**
total fat	**4 g**
saturated fat	**trace**
cholesterol	**0 mg**
carbohydrate	**9 g**
dietary fiber	**3 g**
sodium	**326 mg**

R.D.I. Vit A 35%, E 11%, C 43%, Folate 36%, Ca 9% (101 mg), Iron 15%, Zinc 5%.

Canada's Food Guide Serving:
2¼

Spices, garlic, red pepper flakes and lemon add terrific flavor to this quick vegetable dish. My husband prefers it with 1/4 tsp (1 mL) red pepper flakes. However, he likes most dishes hotter than I do.

1 tbsp	vegetable oil	15 mL
1 tsp	cumin seeds	5 mL
4	cloves garlic, minced	4
1 tsp	ground coriander	5 mL
1/4 cup	water	50 mL
1 tbsp	fresh lemon juice	15 mL
1 tsp	granulated sugar	5 mL
1/2 tsp	salt	2 mL
Pinch	red pepper flakes	Pinch
6 cups	thinly sliced cabbage	1.5 L
3 cups	thinly sliced spinach	750 mL

1 In heavy saucepan, heat oil over medium heat. Add cumin seeds; cook until sizzling. Stir in garlic and coriander; cook, stirring, for 30 seconds. Add water, lemon juice, sugar, salt and red pepper flakes.

2 Stir in cabbage and bring to simmer; cover and simmer for 15 to 20 minutes or until cabbage is tender.

3 Stir in spinach; cook for 2 minutes or until wilted. *Makes 4 servings.*

Make ahead: Through step 2 for up to 2 hours.

Spinach with Tomatoes and Cumin

*The dynamic flavors of cumin, ground coriander and fresh ginger
liven up spinach. This side dish goes well with grilled or roasted meats,
chicken or fish and mashed potatoes or rice dishes.*

1 lb	fresh spinach (or 10 oz/300 g bag), trimmed	500 g
1-1/2 tsp	butter	7 mL
1/2 tsp	ground cumin or cumin seeds	2 mL
1/4 tsp	ground coriander	1 mL
2 tbsp	chopped onion	25 mL
1	clove garlic, minced	1
1 tsp	grated gingerroot	5 mL
1	small tomato, seeded and finely chopped	1
Pinch	salt	Pinch
2 tbsp	1% sour cream	25 mL

1 Remove tough stems from spinach; rinse and shake off excess water. In saucepan,
cover and cook spinach over medium heat, with just the water clinging to leaves, for
3 minutes or until wilted; drain well and chop.

2 Meanwhile, in nonstick skillet, melt butter over medium heat; cook cumin and
coriander, stirring, for 1 minute. Add onion and garlic; cook, stirring occasionally, for
2 minutes or until tender.

3 Add ginger, tomato and salt; cook for 1 minute or until heated through. Stir in
spinach, then sour cream. *Makes 3 servings.*

Make ahead: Through step 2 for up to 2 hours.

Per serving:

calories	**59**
protein	**4 g**
total fat	**2 g**
saturated fat	1 g
cholesterol	6 mg
carbohydrate	**7 g**
dietary fiber	**3 g**
sodium	**90 mg**

R.D.I. Vit A 73%, E 9%, C 22%,
Folate 56%, Ca 13% (142 mg), Iron 24%,
Zinc 8%.

Canada's Food Guide Serving:
1¾ 🥕

Menopause on the Menu

If you are a woman in your forties or early fifties and are suffering from the discomforts of mid-life menstrual and menopausal symptoms, you may have wondered if therapies like vitamin B6, dong quai and oil of evening primrose can help. The symptoms associated with perimenopause (the years before menstruation ceases) stem primarily from fluctuating levels of estrogen. Most therapies either directly replace the estrogen or treat the symptoms brought on by its decline.

The Soybean Connection

The fact that Japanese women don't suffer from the menopausal complaints of American women has been linked to their diet, which is high in soybean foods. Soybeans contain compounds known as isoflavones, which are converted during digestion to phytoestrogens or plant estrogens. Preliminary evidence suggests that these plant estrogens may be useful in relieving the discomfort of hot flashes, night sweats and vaginal dryness.

Herbs such as fenugreek, gotu kola, sarsaparilla, licorice root and wild yam root are also said to contain estrogen-like substances, but there is little evidence to confirm or challenge the usefulness of these therapies.

HEALTHY EATING TIPS: Help for the Symptoms of PMS and Menopause

Women today have a variety of therapies, both traditional and alternative, available to help them through the perimenopause and the menopausal years. Whatever therapies you try, these diet and lifestyle tips are bound to help you cope with some of the common symptoms and discomforts.

- Adopt a healthy eating pattern.
- Include more vegetarian dishes in your meals, especially more soybean-based products such as tofu.
- Avoid caffeine if you are experiencing sleep problems or breast tenderness.
- Limit your salt intake. Recent evidence concludes that water isn't retained premenstrually but simply shifts around, a phenomena unrelated to the influences of salt. However, eating less salt is still a healthy choice.

- Avoid alcohol, especially red wine, beer, rum, rye, brandy and sherry if you suffer from headaches and depression. These symptoms may also improve by avoiding chocolate, aged cheese, nuts, aspartame, onions, tomatoes, mushrooms, nitrites and monosodium glutamate.
- Eat smaller and more frequent meals.

Other Nutrition-Related Therapies

Other nutrition-related therapies are thought to act by increasing levels of neurotransmitters in the brain, particularly serotonin. Low levels of serotonin have been linked to hot flashes, mood swings, irritability, sleep problems and fluid retention. At this time, none of these therapies has proved effective. They are discussed here only as a caution against popular self-help therapies.

- Vitamin B6: This vitamin can cause nerve damage. Long-term use of 50 to 100 mg daily is likely safe; never take more than 200 mg daily.
- Vitamin A: Vitamin A is relatively safe up to 8000 Retinol Equivalents except during pregnancy. Excess vitamin A causes birth defects and should never be taken if there is any chance of pregnancy occurring.
- Vitamin E: Vitamin E in dosages of 300 IU is relatively safe but should not be taken when on anticoagulant (blood thinner) medication. Never self-medicate with amounts in excess of 800 IU.
- Calcium and magnesium: Both calcium and magnesium are relatively safe when taken sensibly. For premenstrual and menopausal symptoms, calcium supplements of 1000 mg daily are common. If you take magnesium, limit the supplement to 300 to 600 mg daily.
- Oil of evening primrose: Oil of evening primrose is safe but costly and sometimes causes diarrhea.
- Dong quai: The active ingredients in dong quai are coumarins, naturally occurring chemicals that are harmful in larger doses. For this reason, it is not advisable to use dong quai.
- Ginseng: Some types of ginseng can increase the risk of the very symptoms women are trying to avoid: nervousness, sleeplessness, diarrhea, hypertension, even uterine bleeding.

Poultry and Meat

Ginger Chicken

Asian Chicken

Mexican Chicken with Cumin and Garlic

Spicy Baked Chicken with Tomato Salsa

Thai Chicken Curry in Coconut Milk

Baked Chicken Breasts with Mango Chutney Sauce

Chicken, Italian Sausage and Sweet Pepper Skewers

Chicken, Spinach and Dried Cranberry Phyllo Pie

Sesame Herb Chicken

Provençal Saffron Chicken

Romaine Salad with Grilled Lemon Chicken

Roasted Chicken, Fennel and Sweet Potatoes

Cornish Hens with Porcini Mushrooms and Basil Stuffing

Cranberry-Glazed Turkey Breast

Turkey Potato Patties

Grilled Turkey Scaloppini in Citrus Ginger Sauce

Turkey Scaloppini with Tomato and Herbs

Ginger Beef and Broccoli Stir-Fry

Szechuan Green Beans and Beef with Rice

Salsa Meat Loaf

Picadillo

Beef Fajitas

Mexican Pork Loin Roast

Chinese Barbecued Pork Tenderloin

Thai Pork and Vegetable Curry with Fresh Basil

Rack of Lamb with Wine Sauce and Cucumber Mint Raita

Greek Marinated Leg of Lamb

Nutritional Notes

Cholesterol: "Help! The Doctor Says My Cholesterol Is Too High"

Red Meats: "Red Meat and Health"

Iron: "Iron-Clad Advice"

Help! The Doctor Says My Cholesterol Is Too High

Unhealthy levels of cholesterol or triglycerides in the blood are right up there with smoking, high blood pressure and lack of physical activity as risk factors for heart disease and stroke. Fortunately, changes in your diet can significantly lower the risk.

A Primer on Blood Fats: Cholesterol and Triglycerides

- LDL-C, or Low Density Lipoprotein Cholesterol, is the so-called bad kind of cholesterol. It clogs arteries, causes high blood pressure, heart attacks and stroke. The lower LDL-C, the better.
- HDL-C, or High Density Lipoprotein Cholesterol, is a good form of cholesterol. A high reading is a sign that cholesterol is being delivered to the liver, where it is processed and excreted as it should be. The higher HDL-C, the better.
- TC, or Total Cholesterol, is the sum of LDL-C and HDL-C. Although a low TC is generally good news, you can still be at increased risk for heart attack and stroke if your HDL-C is low as well.
- TG, or triglycerides, are a type of blood fat that, like LDL-C, can increase the risk of heart disease, particularly in women. High triglyceride levels tend to go hand in hand with being overweight, alcohol consumption, high blood pressure, low HDL-C levels and diabetes.

HEALTHY EATING TIPS: Lowering High Blood Cholesterol

- Cut back on total amount of fat in your diet, particularly saturated and trans fat (hydrogenated or partially hydrogenated vegetable oil), by following the Lower-Fat Tips throughout this cookbook. To lower elevated blood fats, no more than 25% of your day's calories should come from fat. To get 25% or less of the day's calories from fat, most men should limit fat intake to 75 grams or less, and most women should limit fat intake to 53 grams or less.
- Eat lots of fiber, especially soluble fiber, which helps to lower LDL cholesterol. Whole grain foods, vegetables, fruits and legumes (dried beans, peas and lentils) are high in fiber. (See page 266.)

What's Healthy?

These are commonly accepted benchmarks for healthy blood levels of cholesterol and triglycerides:

- **LDL-C** less than 3.4 mmol\L
- **HDL-C** more than 0.9 mmol\L
- **TC** less than 5.2 mmol\L
- **TG** less than 2.3 mmol\L

Levels of TC, LDL-C and TG above these levels or a HDL-C below this level are associated with increasing risk for heart disease.

- When a recipe calls for fat, use a little soft margarine or an oil high in either polyunsaturates or monounsaturates instead of butter or shortening. Good choices in oil are olive, canola, safflower, sunflower and corn.
- Restrict the cholesterol in your diet to less than 250 mg a day. The main foods to avoid are organ meats, such as liver, and whole eggs. Eat no more than 2 whole eggs per week, although cholesterol-free egg whites can be used in food preparation. Two egg whites combined with 1 tsp (5 mL) oil can replace 1 whole egg in most recipes.
- If your triglycerides are high as well, avoid all forms of sugar (white and brown sugar, honey, syrup) and alcohol since sugar and alcohol, once digested, are readily converted to triglycerides. Eating more fish rich in omega-3 fat (see page 203) may also help lower blood triglycerides.
- If you are overweight, lose weight. Even small losses can make a big difference. (See page 16.)

HEALTHY EATING TIPS: Raising the Good HDL-Cholesterol

Raising HDL-C is more difficult than lowering TC and LDL-C but it's worth trying if your HDL-C is too low. Follow the same advice for lowering LDL-C with special attention to these points and exceptions:

- Exercise every day. It's more important than ever.
- Choose margarines and oils like olive and canola oil that contain mostly monounsaturated fat rather than oils like safflower, sunflower and corn oil that contain mostly polyunsaturates. Monounsaturated fat doesn't lower HDL-C, whereas polyunsaturates do.
- Women who are at menopause might consider hormone replacement therapy since estrogen raises HDL-C levels.
- Some people may benefit from an alcoholic drink. See page 34 for more details.

Lower-Fat Tip

To reduce fat intake from meat and poultry, reduce portion sizes. Have a 4-oz (125 g) steak instead of an 8-oz (250 g) steak. Have one pork chop or chicken kebab, not two. Make smaller hamburger patties.

Chicken, Italian Sausage and Sweet Pepper Skewers

The sausages in this great summer barbecue dish complement the chicken and colorful vegetables. I usually serve this over rice.

Cooking Tip

I use wooden skewers rather than metal because food sticks to the wood and doesn't slip when turned. To prevent charring, soak wooden skewers in water for 30 minutes before using.

Nutrition Tip

Sweet red and yellow peppers are very high in vitamin C.

3	small hot Italian sausages (12 oz/375 g)	3
1 lb	boneless skinless chicken breasts	500 g
2	medium sweet peppers (red, yellow or green)	2
2	small yellow or green zucchini	2
Half	red onion or one-quarter Spanish onion	Half
1/4 cup	balsamic vinegar	50 mL
1 tbsp	Dijon mustard	15 mL
2	cloves garlic, minced	2
1/4 tsp	each dried thyme, basil and pepper	1 mL
1 tbsp	olive oil	15 mL

1 Prick sausages all over with sharp knife. Place in saucepan and pour in enough water to cover; bring to boil. Reduce heat and simmer for 15 minutes or until firm; drain. Cut sausages and chicken into 1-inch (2.5 cm) pieces.

2 Core and seed sweet peppers; cut into 1-inch (2.5 cm) pieces. Remove ends from zucchini; cut into 3/4-inch (2 cm) thick slices. Cut onion into 3 or 4 pieces; separate into 1-1/2-inch (4 cm) thick wedges.

3 In shallow dish, combine sausages, chicken, peppers, zucchini and onion. In measuring cup, whisk together vinegar, mustard, garlic, thyme, basil and pepper; whisk in oil. Pour over chicken mixture and toss to mix. Cover and refrigerate for at least 2 hours or for up to 8 hours.

4 Alternating ingredients, thread sausage, chicken, peppers, onion and zucchini onto six 12-inch (30 cm) soaked wooden skewers.

5 Place on greased grill over medium heat. Baste with any remaining marinade. Close lid and cook, turning occasionally, for 10 to 15 minutes or until chicken is no longer pink inside. *Makes 6 servings.*

Make ahead: Through step 3 for up to 8 hours. Through step 4 for up to 1 hour.

Per serving:

calories	234
protein	26 g
total fat	9 g
saturated fat	3 g
cholesterol	68 mg
carbohydrate	10 g
dietary fiber	2 g
sodium	402 mg

R.D.I. Vit A 13%, E 3%, C 110%, Folate 10%, Ca 3% (29 mg), Iron 10%, Zinc 13%.

Canada's Food Guide Serving:
1¾ 🥕 1½ 🍗

Hoisin-Glazed Sea Bass

All my tasters loved this dish, whether it was made with swordfish, tuna,
halibut or salmon; in the oven, on the grill or in the microwave.
Strips of green onion or chives add a fresh colorful garnish to the plate.

Hoisin-Glazed Salmon Steaks

My favorite way to barbecue salmon is to simply spread it with hoisin sauce. Grill over medium-high heat, with lid down, for 3 to 5 minutes per side or until fish flakes when tested with fork.

Cooking Tip

For very tender, moist results, microwave the Hoisin-Glazed Sea Bass at High for 5 minutes instead of grilling or baking.

2 tbsp	hoisin sauce	25 mL
1 tsp	minced gingerroot	5 mL
1 tsp	sesame oil	5 mL
1/4 tsp	chili paste (optional)	1 mL
4	sea bass fillets, 1-inch (2.5 cm) thick (4 oz/125 g each)	4

1 In small bowl, mix together hoisin sauce, ginger, oil, and chili paste (if using).

2 Spread over each side of fish. Place on greased grill or on broiler pan or on baking sheet. Grill over medium heat with lid down, basting occasionally with any remaining hoisin mixture, for 5 minutes. Turn and grill for another 5 minutes or until fish flakes easily when tested with fork. (Or bake in 425°F/220°C oven for 10 minutes.) *Makes 4 servings.*

Per serving:

calories	**135**
protein	**21 g**
total fat	**3 g**
saturated fat	**1 g**
cholesterol	**47 mg**
carbohydrate	**4 g**
dietary fiber	**trace**
sodium	**207 mg**

R.D.I. Vit A 6%, Folate 3%,
Ca 1% (14 mg), Iron 3%, Zinc 5%.

Canada's Food Guide Serving:

1 ❯

Red Snapper with Lime Coriander Marinade

These moist, flavorful fillets are easy to prepare and quick to cook.
You can also substitute sea bass, rainbow trout, grouper or swordfish fillets.
Serve with wedges of lime and garnish plate with sprigs of coriander.

1-1/2 lb	red snapper fillets	750 g
1/4 cup	chopped fresh coriander (cilantro)	50 mL
	grated lime rind from 1 medium lime	
1/4 cup	fresh lime juice	50 mL
2 tbsp	olive oil	25 mL
2	cloves garlic, minced	2
1 tsp	minced canned or fresh green chilies (optional)	5 mL
1/4 tsp	each salt and pepper	1 mL

Grilled Fillets with Lime Coriander Marinade

Prepare through step 1. Grease and preheat barbecue to medium heat; grill fillets for 3 to 5 minutes on each side (time will vary depending on thickness of fish and temperature of barbecue and weather if outside) or until fish is opaque and flakes easily when tested with fork.

1 Place fillets in 8-inch (2 L) square baking dish. Whisk together coriander, lime rind and juice, oil, garlic, chilies, salt and pepper; pour over fillets. Cover and marinate for 30 minutes.

2 Bake in 425°F (220°C) oven for 15 minutes or until fish flakes easily when tested with fork. *Makes 4 servings.*

Per serving:

calories	**204**
protein	**35 g**
total fat	**6 g**
saturated fat	**1 g**
cholesterol	**62 mg**
carbohydrate	**1 g**
sodium	**145 mg**

R.D.I. Vit A 5%, E 4%, C 7%, Folate 4%, Ca 5% (56 mg), Iron 3%, Zinc 7%.

Canada's Food Guide Serving:
1¾)

Fish

Eat fish at least twice a week. Fish is either very low in fat or contains healthy omega-3 fats.

Raw Fish Alert

Is raw fish sushi safe to eat? There is always a risk of food poisoning or parasitic (worms) invasion with raw fish. Marinating does not kill bacteria or parasites. Reputable sushi bars use previously frozen fish for raw fish dishes since freezing kills parasites. Buy only commercially frozen fish if you prepare sushi at home. According to Health Canada, raw or undercooked shellfish such as mussels, clams or oysters are high-risk foods.

Per serving:

calories	178
protein	27 g
total fat	6 g
saturated fat	1 g
cholesterol	45 mg
carbohydrate	5 g
dietary fiber	1 g
sodium	349 mg

R.D.I. Vit A 7%, E 6%, C 17%, Folate 11%, Ca 4% (49 mg), Iron 11%, Zinc 11%.

Canada's Food Guide Serving:

½ 2)

Monkfish with Sun-Dried Tomatoes,
Capers and Basil

Monkfish is a deliciously moist fish that is wonderful in this easy Provençal-type recipe. If unavailable, use fresh cod, sea bass or halibut fillets. (I tried it with frozen cod fillets and prefer the fresh.)

1/3 cup	dry-packed sun-dried tomatoes	75 mL
2	cloves garlic	2
1/2 cup	lightly packed fresh Italian parsley	125 mL
1/4 cup	lightly packed fresh basil leaves	50 mL
1 tbsp	capers, drained	15 mL
6	black olives, pitted and chopped	6
3	anchovies, chopped	3
1-1/2 tsp	olive oil	7 mL
1-1/2 lb	monkfish fillets, skinless	750 g

1 Cover tomatoes with hot water; soak for 15 minutes or until softened. Drain.

2 In food processor, combine tomatoes, garlic, parsley, basil, capers, olives, anchovies and oil; chop coarsely.

3 Place fish on lightly greased baking sheet; evenly spread tomato mixture over fish.

4 Bake in 375°F (190°C) oven for 10 to 15 minutes or until opaque throughout. (Time will vary depending on thickness of fish.) *Makes 4 servings.*

Make ahead: Through step 3, cover and refrigerate for up to 4 hours.

Mediterranean Spring Dinner

Monkfish with Sun-Dried Tomatoes, Capers and Basil (this page)

Leek and Rice Pilaf (page 116)

Asparagus with Shaved Parmesan (page 137)

French Lemon Tart (page 282)

Oven-Fried Fish Fillets

Serve this pleasing family supper with Sesame-Spiced Oven-Fried Potatoes (page 144). You can use almost any white fish fillets. If using frozen, be sure to thaw them before cooking.

1/2 cup	fine dry bread crumbs	125 mL
1-1/2 tsp	dried Italian herb seasoning (or basil and oregano)	7 mL
1 tsp	grated lemon rind	5 mL
1/2 tsp	each salt and pepper	2 mL
1	egg or 2 egg whites	1
1 tsp	water	5 mL
1 lb	fish fillets (halibut or cod)	500 g
1 tsp	vegetable oil	5 mL

1 In shallow dish, stir together bread crumbs, herb seasoning, lemon rind, salt and pepper.

2 In small bowl, beat egg or whites with water.

3 Dip fillets into egg; dip into bread crumb mixture to coat both sides.

4 Spread oil on baking sheet; place in 450°F (230°C) oven for 30 seconds. Place fish in single layer on hot baking sheet. Bake in top half of oven for 4 minutes; turn and bake for another 4 minutes for 1/2-inch (1 cm) thick fillets, another 6 minutes for 1-inch (2.5 cm) thick fillets. *Makes 4 servings.*

Cooking Tip

Oven-frying reduces the fat but keeps the coating and flavor of fried fish. In place of the hot oil in a frying pan, use a teaspoon (5 mL) of oil on a baking sheet.

Toaster Oven Method

This dish cooks fine in a toaster oven. Be sure to pre-heat oven. Cook two pieces of fish at a time for 10 minutes or until fish flakes when tested with a fork.

Per serving:

calories	198
protein	27 g
total fat	5 g
cholesterol	36 mg
carbohydrate	10 g
dietary fiber	1 g
sodium	492 mg

R.D.I. Vit A 5%, E 12%, C 2%, Folate 7%, Ca 8% (92 mg), Iron 14%, Zinc 7%.

Canada's Food Guide Serving:

½ 🌾   1¼ ▶

Shrimp Provençal Casserole

The Provençal flavorings of garlic, parsley and fresh basil make this a well-liked make-ahead dish. Extra large or large shrimp work best. Serve with Spinach Salad with Walnut Vinaigrette (page 38) and crusty bread.

Cholesterol-Lowering Tip

Yes, shrimp do contain some cholesterol, but because they are also so low in calories and fat, they can be eaten in moderation on a cholesterol-lowering diet.

1 tbsp	olive oil	15 mL
1-1/4 cups	long-grain converted rice	300 mL
3/4 cup	chopped fresh parsley	175 mL
1/3 cup	chopped fresh basil or 2 tsp (10 mL) dried	75 mL
1	large onion, chopped	1
1	sweet green pepper, chopped	1
6	large cloves garlic, minced	6
6 cups	halved mushrooms (1 lb/500 g)	1.5 L
1	can (28 oz/796 mL) tomatoes, chopped	1
1/4 tsp	crushed red pepper flakes	1 mL
1-1/2 lb	large peeled shrimp (raw or cooked)	750 g
3/4 cup	freshly grated Parmesan cheese	175 mL

1 In saucepan, heat 1/2 tsp (2 mL) of the oil over medium heat; cook rice, stirring, for 1 minute. Add 2-1/2 cups (625 mL) boiling water; cover, reduce heat and simmer for 15 to 20 minutes or until water is absorbed and rice is still slightly firm. Sprinkle with 1/4 cup (50 mL) of the parsley, half of the basil, and salt and pepper to taste. Spread in greased 13- x 9-inch (3 L) baking dish.

2 In large nonstick skillet, heat remaining oil over medium heat; cook onion and green pepper, stirring occasionally, for 5 minutes. Add two-thirds of the garlic and the mushrooms; increase heat to high and cook, stirring often, for 5 minutes or until vegetables are tender.

3 Add tomatoes and red pepper flakes; bring to boil. Reduce heat to medium; simmer, uncovered and stirring occasionally, for 10 to 15 minutes or until sauce-like consistency. Stir in shrimp, half of the remaining parsley, half of the cheese and remaining basil. Spoon over rice.

Per serving:

calories	400
protein	34 g
total fat	9 g
saturated fat	3 g
cholesterol	182 mg
carbohydrate	45 g
dietary fiber	4 g
sodium	626 mg

R.D.I. Vit A 18%, E 10%, C 58%, Folate 18%, Ca 25% (277 mg), Iron 32%, Zinc 29%.

Canada's Food Guide Serving:

1¼ 🌾 2¾ 🥕 ¼ 🥛 1 🍗

Fresh Fruit, Granola and Yogurt Trifle

Daphna Rabinovitch, associate food director at Canadian Living *magazine, developed this perfect brunch or special breakfast dish. She uses mango, fresh pineapple, kiwifruit, grapes and strawberries, which are wonderful together. Use fresh fruit in season and serve as part of a buffet or as the main dish or to end the meal.*

1	orange	1
2 cups	low-fat granola	500 mL
3 cups	2% plain yogurt	750 mL
1/3 cup	granulated sugar	75 mL
1/3 cup	dried cherries (optional)	75 mL
4 cups	fresh fruit*	1 L

1 Grate rind or zest from orange. Cut off all white membranes; cut orange into segments and set aside.

2 Spoon granola into 8-cup (2 L) glass serving bowl. Combine yogurt, sugar and grated orange rind; reserve 1/2 cup (125 mL). Spoon remaining yogurt mixture over granola. Sprinkle with dried cherries (if using). Cover and refrigerate for 1 hour.

3 Just before serving, spoon fresh fruit over top. Drizzle with reserved yogurt mixture. *Makes 8 servings.*

Make ahead: Cover and refrigerate prepared fruit for up to 1 day. Through step 2, cover and refrigerate for up to 4 hours.

* Use 1/2 cup (125 mL) sliced peeled mango, 1 cup (250 mL) cubed peeled fresh pineapple, 2 kiwifruit, peeled, halved and sliced, 1 cup (250 mL) halved seedless grapes, 3/4 cup (175 mL) sliced strawberries, 1 orange, in segments.

Easy Granola

In large bowl, con
(1.25 L) quick-co
1 cup (250 mL) w
1/2 cup (125 mL)
germ, 1/4 cup (50
chopped almonds
and sunflower se
(175 mL) liquid h
2 lightly greased t
squeeze together
clumps. Bake in 3
oven for 20 minu
golden brown, st
granola will brow
1-1/2 cups (375 m
cool completely. S
containers. *Makes*

Per serving:
calories
protein
total fat
   saturated fat
   cholesterol
carbohydrate
dietary fiber
sodium
R.D.I. Vit A 6%, E 6%, C
Folate 10%, Ca 19% (211
Zinc 9%.

Canada's Food Guide
¾ 🌾 1 🥕 ½ 🥛

---

4 Combine remaining cheese, chopped garlic and parsley; sprinkle over tomato mixture. Bake, uncovered, in 325°F (160°C) oven for 30 to 40 minutes or until bubbling. *Makes 6 servings.*

Make ahead: Through step 3, but reduce cooking time to 8 minutes; cover and refrigerate for up to 1 day. Increase baking time by 10 to 15 minutes.

Pan-Seared Sea Bass with Red Onion and Lemon

I love sea bass; it's very juicy and rich-tasting. Like most fish, it is best when prepared simply.

4	sea bass fillets, 4 to 5 oz (125 to 150 g) each, skin on	4
	Salt and pepper	
4 tsp	olive oil	20 mL
1/2 cup	thinly sliced red onion	125 mL
2 tbsp	fresh lemon juice	25 mL
3/4 tsp	fennel seeds, crushed	4 mL

1 Sprinkle fillets with salt and pepper to taste. In nonstick skillet, heat 1 tsp (5 mL) of the oil over medium-high heat; cook fillets, skin side down, for 2 minutes. Turn and cook for 2 minutes.

2 Reduce heat to medium. Add onion; cover and cook for 4 minutes or until opaque. Remove fish to warmed plates.

3 Add remaining oil, lemon juice and fennel seeds to skillet; bring to simmer and cook, stirring, for 1 minute or until onion is tender. Season with salt and pepper to taste. Drizzle over fish and top with onion. *Makes 4 servings.*

Per serving:

calories	151
protein	19 g
total fat	7 g
saturated fat	1 g
cholesterol	42 mg
carbohydrate	3 g
dietary fiber	trace
sodium	71 mg

R.D.I. Vit A 5%, E 6%, C 5%,
Folate 4%, Ca 2% (19 mg), Iron 3%,
Zinc 5%.

Canada's Food Guide Serving:
¼ 🥕 1 🐟

Asparagus and Mushroom Gra[...]

This brunch casserole is just as enjoyable as a quiche yet is much[...]
Serve with Carrot Slaw with Radicchio (page 39) or Thai Vegetarian S[...]
Fig and Cottage Cheese Quick Bread (page 245) and Fresh Frui[...]
and Yogurt Trifle (opposite page)

1 lb	asparagus
2 tsp	butter
2	onions, chopped
6 cups	thickly sliced mushrooms (about 1 lb/500 g)
1/3 cup	all-purpose flour
3	eggs
1-1/2 cups	1% or 2% milk
1 tsp	Dijon mustard
1/2 tsp	salt
Pinch	each cayenne pepper and grated nutmeg
1 cup	grated light Swiss-style cheese or Danbo

1 Snap ends off asparagus; cut stalks into 1-inch (2.5 cm) pieces. In [...]
boiling water, cook asparagus until tender-crisp, about 3 minutes.[...]
cold water; dry and set aside.

2 In nonstick skillet, melt butter over medium-high heat; cook onior[...]
occasionally, for 5 minutes. Add mushrooms; cook, stirring often, [...]
about 8 minutes. Sprinkle with flour; cook, stirring, for 1 minute. F[...]

3 In large bowl, beat eggs lightly; whisk in milk, mustard, salt, cayen[...]
Add onion mixture, asparagus and half of the cheese. Pour into gre[...]
(2 L) baking dish, smoothing top. Sprinkle with remaining cheese.[...]
(180°C) oven for 45 to 55 minutes or until set. Broil for 2 minutes.[...]

Make ahead: Through step 1, wrap in paper towels and refrigerate [...]

Per serving:

calories	144
protein	11 g
total fat	6 g
saturated fat	2 g
cholesterol	85 mg
carbohydrate	13 g
dietary fiber	2 g
sodium	247 mg

R.D.I. Vit A 9%, D 15%, E 5%, C 12%,
Folate 35%, Ca 19% (212 mg), Iron 11%,
Zinc 11%.

Canada's Food Guide Serving:
¼ 🌾 1¾ 🥕 ¼ 🥛 ¼ 🍗

Raising Healthy Teenagers

When children become teenagers, parents' influence over their eating habits diminishes. Like many other adolescent attitudes, beliefs and behavior, eating is now much more influenced by the child's peer group.

Faced with their child's changing and sometimes bizarre eating patterns, many parents wonder how to distinguish between behavior that is simply characteristic of a growing independence and habits that may indicate a more serious eating disorder.

For all we know about food and eating these days, some people, adults and children alike, have lost sight of what is a normal, natural way of eating. Many of the typical adolescent eating habits—snacking, skipping breakfast and indulging a well-developed taste for snack food—are no cause for concern on their own.

Healthy Eating Habits Include:

- enjoying food and eating—sometimes with great gusto—without feeling guilty
- eating regularly
- being willing to try new foods, but also being comfortable turning them down
- eating when hungry and stopping when they are full
- generally—if not always—following the basic principles of healthy eating

Warning Signs of Eating Disorders

Eating disorders such as emotional overeating, anorexia and bulimia are distortions in eating accompanied by an underlying emotional difficulty. If you think your child is developing an eating disorder, seek professional medical help.

Be concerned about teenagers who exhibit these warning signs:

- a preoccupation with weight
- a feeling of being "fat" when clearly not overweight
- a preoccupation with food, calories, eating, ritualistic eating patterns
- hiding food
- an obsession with exercise
- periods of starvation followed by binges on high-calorie foods
- denying hunger
- self-induced vomiting (watch for trips to the bathroom after eating)
- evidence that laxatives, diuretics, or diet pills are used
- feelings of guilt or shame about eating
- low self-esteem, feelings of stupidity in a competent, contentious teen
- chronic fatigue, irritability, depression
- complaints about being cold, bloated

Roasted Red Pepper, Onion and Hummus Pita Wrap

This combination is particularly tasty and colorful. Grilled eggplant and zucchini (page 156) would make interesting additions. You can substitute tortillas for the pitas.

3	9-inch (23 cm) pitas	3
3 cups	Spicy Hummus (page 12)	750 mL
1-1/2 cups	thinly sliced red onion	375 mL
6	leaves lettuce, shredded	6
6	leaves raddichio, shredded	6
2	roasted sweet red peppers (page 32), thinly sliced	2
12	black olives, pitted and sliced	12
1/2 cup	whole fresh coriander (cilantro) leaves	125 mL
2 tbsp	chopped pickled hot banana peppers (optional)	25 mL

1 Cut each pita in half to form rounds; evenly spread entire surface of each with hummus.

2 In rows down center, evenly arrange onion, lettuce, raddichio, red peppers, olives, coriander, and hot peppers (if using). Roll up tightly; cut in half on the diagonal. *Makes 6 servings, 2 pieces each.*

Make ahead: Through step 2, wrap in plastic wrap and refrigerate for up to 3 hours.

Lower-Fat Tip

Choose plain breads and rolls for sandwiches. A croissant can contain as much as 15 grams of fat.

Per serving:

calories	306
protein	12 g
total fat	7 g
saturated fat	1 g
cholesterol	0 mg
carbohydrate	51 g
dietary fiber	5 g
sodium	501 mg

R.D.I. Vit A 12%, E 7%, C 93%, Folate 40%, Ca 9% (95 mg), Iron 24%, Zinc 15%.

Canada's Food Guide Serving:

1¼ 🌾 1½ 🥕 1¼ 🍖

Lemon Zucchini Muffins

Grated zucchini adds moistness and texture
to these lemon-spiked muffins.

Lower-Fat Baking Tip
Add grated fruits such as
apple, or vegetables such
as zucchini or carrots, to
muffins or quick-breads to
keep them from drying out.

2 cups	all-purpose flour	500 mL
1 cup	shredded (unpeeled) zucchini	250 mL
1/2 cup	granulated sugar	125 mL
	Coarsely grated rind from 1 large lemon	
1 tsp	each baking powder and baking soda	5 mL
1/2 tsp	salt	2 mL
1	egg	1
3/4 cup	buttermilk or soured milk*	175 mL
1/4 cup	vegetable oil	50 mL
1/4 cup	fresh lemon juice	50 mL

1 Lightly grease or spray nonstick muffin pans with nonstick cooking spray.

2 In large bowl, stir together flour, zucchini, sugar, lemon rind, baking powder, baking soda and salt.

3 In separate bowl, lightly beat egg; whisk in buttermilk, oil and lemon juice. Pour over flour mixture and stir just enough to moisten, being careful not to overmix.

4 Spoon into prepared pans. Bake in 375°F (190°C) oven for 25 to 30 minutes or until tops are golden and firm to the touch. *Makes 12 muffins.*

Make ahead: Store in airtight container for up to 2 days or freeze for up to 2 months.

Per muffin:

calories	164
protein	3 g
total fat	5 g
saturated fat	1 g
cholesterol	18 mg
carbohydrate	26 g
dietary fiber	1 g
sodium	237 mg

R.D.I. Vit A 1%, D 1%, E 10%, C 5%, Folate 4%, Ca 3% (35 mg), Iron 7%, Zinc 3%.

Canada's Food Guide Serving:
1 🌾

* To sour milk, measure 2 tsp (10 mL) lemon juice or vinegar into measuring cup. Add milk to 3/4 cup (175 mL) level; let stand for 5 minutes, then stir.

Strawberry-Glazed Banana Pineapple Muffins

A spoonful of strawberry jam bakes into
the top of these intriguing and nutritious muffins.

2 cups	whole wheat flour	500 mL
1/2 cup	granulated sugar	125 mL
1 tsp	each baking powder and baking soda	5 mL
1/4 tsp	salt	1 mL
1	egg	1
1 cup	mashed bananas	250 mL
1/2 cup	drained crushed unsweetened pineapple	125 mL
1/4 cup	each vegetable oil and milk	50 mL
1 tsp	grated lemon or orange rind	5 mL
1/4 cup	strawberry jam	50 mL

1 Lightly grease or spray nonstick muffin pans with nonstick cooking spray.

2 In large bowl, stir together flour, sugar, baking powder, baking soda and salt.

3 In separate bowl, lightly beat egg; stir in bananas, pineapple, oil, milk and lemon rind. Pour over flour mixture and stir just enough to moisten, being careful not to overmix.

4 Spoon into prepared pans. Top each with dollop of jam. Bake in 400°F (200°C) oven for 20 to 25 minutes or until tops are firm to the touch. *Makes 12 muffins.*

Make ahead: Store in airtight container for up to 2 days or freeze for up to 2 months.

Baking Tip

Lower-fat muffins tend to stick to paper liners. For best results, use a nonstick pan lightly greased or sprayed with a nonstick coating instead.

Fiber-Booster

Whole grain foods add fiber to your diet. Use whole wheat bread, bagels, brown rice and whole wheat pasta. Use more whole grain flour in your baking, too.

Per muffin:	
calories	188
protein	4 g
total fat	5 g
saturated fat	1 g
cholesterol	18 mg
carbohydrate	34 g
dietary fiber	3 g
sodium	179 mg

R.D.I. Vit A 1%, D 2%, E 13%, C 5%, Folate 5%, Ca 3% (29 mg), Iron 7%, Zinc 8%.

Canada's Food Guide Serving:
1 🌾 ¼ 🥕

Cranberry Orange Bran Muffins

I often make these at Christmas when I have cranberries
in the refrigerator or freezer.

1 cup	wheat bran	250 mL
3/4 cup	each whole wheat flour and all-purpose flour	175 mL
1/3 cup	packed brown sugar	75 mL
	Grated rind from 1 medium orange	
1-1/2 tsp	baking powder	7 mL
1/2 tsp	baking soda	2 mL
1-1/4 cups	cranberries (fresh or frozen)	300 mL
1	egg	1
1 cup	buttermilk or soured milk*	250 mL
1/4 cup	each vegetable oil and molasses	50 mL

1 Lightly grease or spray nonstick muffin pans with nonstick cooking spray.

2 In large bowl, stir together bran, whole wheat flour, all-purpose flour, sugar, orange rind, baking powder, baking soda and cranberries.

3 In separate bowl, lightly beat egg; stir in buttermilk, oil and molasses. Pour over dry ingredients; stir just until moistened.

4 Spoon into prepared pans. Bake in 375°F (190°C) oven for 20 to 25 minutes or until tops are firm to the touch. *Makes 12 muffins.*

Make ahead: Store in airtight container for up to 3 days or freeze for up to 1 month.

*To sour milk, measure 1 tbsp (15 mL) lemon juice or vinegar into measuring cup. Add milk to 1 cup (250 mL) level; let stand for 5 minutes, then stir.

Lower-Fat Tip

Buttermilk is wonderful in lower-fat baking because it helps to make muffins, biscuits and breads tender. And, contrary to its name, it is low in fat.

Fiber-Booster

One of the best opportunities to get at least one-third of your day's fiber is at breakfast. Take advantage of the many high-fiber cereals available. To ensure your cereal is high in fiber, check the nutrition information panel on the side of your cereal box. Include some fruit too: raisins, prunes, a banana or an orange.

Per muffin:

calories	168
protein	4 g
total fat	6 g
saturated fat	1 g
cholesterol	19 mg
carbohydrate	28 g
dietary fiber	4 g
sodium	102 mg

R.D.I. Vit A 2%, D 5%, E 12%, C 7%, Folate 4%, Ca 6% (70 mg), Iron 12%, Zinc 9%.

Canada's Food Guide Serving:
1 🌾

Fig and Cottage Cheese Quick Bread

I first tasted the delightful combination of fig and anise in bread from Tarro Bakery in Vancouver. This easy-to-make breakfast or tea bread is especially good toasted and spread with preserves or marmalade. Instead of figs, you can use chopped dates, prunes or apricots.

2 cups	all-purpose flour	500 mL
2 tbsp	granulated sugar	25 mL
1 tbsp	baking powder	15 mL
1/2 tsp	salt	2 mL
1/2 tsp	aniseed (optional)	2 mL
1 cup	chopped dried figs	250 mL
3/4 cup	2% cottage cheese	175 mL
2 tbsp	vegetable oil	25 mL
1	egg	1
1	egg white	1
2 tsp	milk	10 mL

1 In bowl, stir together flour, sugar, baking powder, salt, and aniseed (if using); stir in figs.

2 In food processor, purée cottage cheese; mix in oil, egg and egg white. Pour over flour mixture; stir just until shaggy dough forms. Gather into ball.

3 Transfer to lightly floured surface (dough may be sticky); knead 2 or 3 times or just until dough holds together. Place on greased baking sheet; flatten into 8-inch (20 cm) round. Brush top with milk. Bake in 350°F (180°C) oven for 35 minutes or until cake tester inserted in center comes out clean. Let stand for 20 minutes.
Makes 16 slices.

Make ahead: Wrap and store at room temperature for up to 1 day.

Lower-Fat Tip

Use puréed cottage cheese or yogurt or buttermilk instead of some of the butter or oil in a quick-bread.

Nutrition Tip

Spread toast with marmalade or another preserve and you won't miss the butter or margarine.

Per slice:

calories	122
protein	4 g
total fat	3 g
saturated fat	trace
cholesterol	14 mg
carbohydrate	21 g
dietary fiber	2 g
sodium	172 mg

R.D.I. Vit A 1%, D 1%, E 4%, C 2%, Folate 2%, Ca 4% (49 mg), Iron 7%, Zinc 3%.

Canada's Food Guide Serving:
1 ｜ ¾

Focaccia

*Warm from the oven, salt-and-herb-topped focaccia bread is wonderful.
I like to use a little whole wheat flour for texture and color, even though focaccia
is usually made just with all-purpose flour.*

**Food Processor
Focaccia**

Pulse dough ingredients
together in food processor
until mixed, then process
on High for 2 minutes or
until in ball and smooth
and elastic. Continue with
rising as in recipe.

Cooking Tip

Check the "best before" date
on the yeast you use. There
are a number of kinds of yeast.
This recipe was developed
using quick-rising yeast which
you add to the flour (other
kinds you add to warm water).
Be sure the water is hot.

Per piece:

calories	121
protein	3 g
total fat	3 g
saturated fat	trace
cholesterol	trace
carbohydrate	20 g
dietary fiber	1 g
sodium	251 mg

R.D.I. Vit E 4%, Folate 5%,
Ca 1% (11 mg), Iron 8%, Zinc 5%.

Canada's Food Guide Serving:
1¼ 🌾

(246)

2 cups	all-purpose flour	500 mL
1/2 cup	whole wheat flour	125 mL
1	pkg (8 g) quick-rising yeast (or 1 tbsp/15 mL)	1
2 tsp	crumbled dried rosemary	10 mL
1 tsp	salt	5 mL
1 cup	hot water or hot milk (120 to 130°F/50 to 55°C)	250 mL
2 tbsp	extra-virgin olive oil	25 mL
1 tsp	granulated sugar	5 mL

Topping:

1 tsp	extra-virgin olive oil	5 mL
1 tsp	each dried Italian herb seasoning and dried rosemary	5 mL
1/2 tsp	coarse salt	2 mL
1/4 tsp	coarsely ground pepper	1 mL

1 In large bowl, combine all-purpose flour, whole wheat flour, yeast, rosemary and
salt. Combine water, oil and sugar; pour over flour mixture. Using wooden spoon,
stir until dough begins to come together and rough ball forms.

2 Turn out dough onto lightly floured surface; knead for about 10 minutes or until
smooth and elastic. Place in lightly greased bowl, turning to grease all over. Cover
with plastic wrap; let rest in warm place for 1 hour.

3 Turn out dough onto lightly floured surface; pat and stretch into 11- x 10-inch
(28 x 25 cm) rectangle, about 1 inch (2.5 cm) thick. Transfer to lightly floured baking
sheet; press back of spoon into dough to create "dimples".

4 Topping: Spread oil over dough. Cover lightly with plastic wrap; let stand at room
temperature for 30 minutes.

5 Sprinkle dough with Italian herbs, rosemary, salt and pepper. Bake in 400°F (200°C)
oven for 15 to 20 minutes or until golden brown and bread sounds hollow when
tapped. Let cool slightly on pan on rack before cutting. *Makes 12 pieces.*

Festive Fruit Soda Bread

I never seem to have enough time to make a Christmas or Easter yeast bread,
but I like this bread just as much — and I can prepare it in only 5 minutes.

Lower-Fat Tip

Any combination of dried
fruits works well in this
recipe. If raisins or currants
are hard, pour boiling water
over them and let them
stand for 10 minutes to
plump, then drain thoroughly.
Hard dried fruits will draw
moisture from the bread
instead of adding juiciness.

4 cups	all-purpose flour	1 L
3 tbsp	granulated sugar	50 mL
1 tbsp	baking powder	15 mL
1 tsp	baking soda	5 mL
1/2 tsp	salt	2 mL
1/3 cup	each raisins, currants, mixed candied fruit and chopped figs	75 mL
1	egg	1
1-3/4 cups	buttermilk	425 mL
3 tbsp	vegetable oil	50 mL
	Grated rind from 1 medium orange	
Glaze:		
1/2 cup	icing sugar	125 mL
1 tbsp	fresh orange juice	15 mL

1 In bowl, stir together flour, sugar, baking powder, baking soda and salt; stir in raisins, currants, mixed candied fruit and figs.

2 In separate bowl, lightly beat egg; whisk in buttermilk, oil and orange rind. Pour over flour mixture and stir just until combined.

3 Transfer to lightly floured surface; knead 10 times or just until dough holds together. Place on greased baking sheet; flatten into 9-inch (23 cm) circle. Bake in 350°F (180°C) oven for 45 to 50 minutes or until toothpick inserted in center comes out clean; let cool on rack for 5 minutes.

4 Glaze: Mix icing sugar with orange juice until smooth; spread over warm bread. Cut into wedges or slices. *Makes 20 slices.*

Make ahead: Wrap and store at room temperature for up to 1 day or wrap again with foil and freeze for up to 1 month.

Per slice:

calories	**174**
protein	**4 g**
total fat	**3 g**
saturated fat	trace
cholesterol	11 mg
carbohydrate	**34 g**
dietary fiber	**2 g**
sodium	**185 mg**

R.D.I. Vit A 1%, D 1%, E 5%, C 5%,
Folate 3%, Ca 5% (57 mg), Iron 9%,
Zinc 4%.

Canada's Food Guide Serving:
1¼ 🌾 ½ 🥕

Apple Raisin Spice Loaf

This moist tea loaf is a good choice for an evening snack or at brunch for dessert along with fruit. It also makes a nice treat in a packed lunch.

2 cups	all-purpose flour	500 mL
2 tsp	each cinnamon and baking powder	10 mL
1 tsp	baking soda	5 mL
1/2 tsp	each ground ginger, nutmeg, allspice and salt	2 mL
1 cup	raisins	250 mL
1/4 cup	butter, softened	50 mL
3/4 cup	granulated sugar	175 mL
1	egg	1
1	egg white	1
2/3 cup	unsweetened applesauce	150 mL
1/2 cup	1% or 2% plain yogurt	125 mL
2 tsp	pure vanilla	10 mL

Fiber-Booster
Add 1/4 cup (50 mL) All-Bran or other high-fiber cereal (one with more than 4 grams of fiber per serving) to your favorite cereal. Sprinkle cereal or yogurt with raisins or other dried fruits or with sunflower seeds.

1 Spray 9- x 5-inch (2 L) loaf pan with nonstick cooking spray.

2 In large bowl, stir together flour, cinnamon, baking powder, baking soda, ginger, nutmeg, allspice, salt and raisins.

3 In separate bowl, using electric mixer, beat butter with sugar until combined; beat in egg and egg white until fluffy. Stir in applesauce, yogurt and vanilla. Pour over flour mixture and stir just until combined. Spoon into pan.

4 Bake in 350°F (180°C) oven for 50 to 60 minutes or until cake tester inserted in center comes out clean. Let cool in pan on rack for 10 minutes. Remove from pan and let cool completely on rack. *Makes 1 loaf, about 18 slices.*

Make ahead: Wrap and store at room temperature for up to 3 days or freeze for up to 1 month.

Per slice:

calories	149
protein	3 g
total fat	3 g
saturated fat	2 g
cholesterol	19 mg
carbohydrate	28 g
dietary fiber	1 g
sodium	197 mg

R.D.I. Vit A 3%, D 1%, E 2%, C 2%, Folate 2%, Ca 3% (38 mg), Iron 7%, Zinc 3%.

Canada's Food Guide Serving:
1 🌾 ½ 🥕

Helping Kids to a Healthy Weight

Preventive Strategies

If your children aren't overweight, it is easier to overlook the importance of healthy eating and being active. But the habits developed in childhood are critical to maintaining a healthy weight as adults. All children, fat or thin, need to learn to choose a healthy diet, to eat appropriate quantities of food, to enjoy sweet and snack foods in moderation and to be physically active every day.

For the most part, Canadian children are a healthy lot, but a disturbing weight-gaining trend has some health experts worried. Overweight children, like overweight adults, are more likely to suffer more physical problems like high blood pressure, respiratory illnesses, diabetes and orthopedic problems. And just like adults, they face the social, emotional and psychological challenges of being fat in a society that reveres thinness. At this point, we can only speculate about why children are getting fatter. Eating habits most certainly play a part. However, if the American experience has any application to Canada, then lack of physical activity is at the top of the list. It is estimated that children today are 40% less active than their parents were.

What can be done about this unhealthy trend? The answer clearly lies in establishing healthy eating and activity patterns early in childhood.

HEALTHY EATING TIPS: Helping the Overweight Child

- Calorie-restricted diets are not recommended; healthy eating is. Establish a healthy eating pattern and encourage more activity for the whole family.
- Make a variety of nutritious food available and allow your child to decide how much he or she wants to eat. Restricting food and denying favorite desserts, treats and snacks can lead to an unhealthy preoccupation with food.
- Encourage your child to participate in activities he or she enjoys. And participate yourself as well. Find activities you and your child enjoy — walking, exploring, skating, tobogganing, swimming, building a snowman, biking. Don't force a child into an activity he or she hates.
- Be sensitive to your child's feelings about weight and the social and emotional burdens. Overweight children often suffer terribly at the hands of other people, and their self-esteem is often low.
- Work with your child to build self-esteem and self-worth through activities and accomplishments unrelated to size, shape and physical performance. Don't send the message that your love and acceptance depend on weight loss.
- Finally, be prepared to accept the fact that not all children will achieve a healthy weight. Nevertheless, these children still need to maintain a pattern of healthy eating and regular physical activity.

Double-Chocolate Cookies

Rich in chocolate flavor, these cookies have less than half the fat of crisp chocolate chip cookies. Cocoa powder contributes a deep chocolate flavor without adding fat. Adding coffee heightens the chocolate flavor.

1 tbsp	each instant coffee granules and pure vanilla	15 mL
1	egg	1
2	egg whites	2
3/4 cup	each granulated sugar and packed brown sugar	175 mL
1/4 cup	butter or margarine, melted	50 mL
3 tbsp	golden corn syrup	50 mL
2 cups	all-purpose flour	500 mL
1/2 cup	unsweetened cocoa powder, sifted	125 mL
1 tbsp	baking powder	15 mL
1/4 tsp	salt	1 mL
1 cup	chocolate chips	250 mL

1 Dissolve coffee granules in vanilla; set aside.

2 In large bowl, using electric mixer, beat egg, egg whites and granulated and brown sugars until light and foamy; beat in butter, corn syrup and coffee mixture.

3 Combine flour, cocoa, baking powder and salt; gradually beat into egg mixture, 1/2 cup (125 mL) at a time, until well mixed. Stir in chocolate chips (mixture will be thick).

4 Drop by tablespoonfuls (15 mL), about 2 inches (5 cm) apart, on nonstick or sprayed baking sheets. Flatten tops with back of spoon. Bake in 350°F (180°C) oven for 8 to 10 minutes or until firm. Let stand on sheets on racks for 2 minutes; transfer to racks to let cool completely. *Makes 60 cookies.*

Make ahead: Store in airtight container for up to 5 days or freeze for up to 3 weeks.

Double-Chocolate Mint Cookies

Substitute 3/4 tsp (4 mL) mint extract for coffee granules; add to batter with vanilla.

Double-Chocolate Orange Cookies

Substitute grated orange rind from 1 orange for coffee granules; add to batter with vanilla.

Per cookie:

calories	**63**
protein	**1 g**
total fat	**2 g**
saturated fat	1 g
cholesterol	6 mg
carbohydrate	**12 g**
dietary fiber	**1 g**
sodium	**36 mg**

R.D.I. Vit A 1%, Ca 1% (12 mg), Iron 3%, Zinc 2%.

Oatmeal and Rice Crisp Squares

Sugar Alert

If you think sugar is to blame for wild behavior in children, you're not alone. However, the evidence—and there's plenty of it—shows that, if anything, sugar has a calming effect. Hyperactive behavior in children has many causes, but it's unlikely that sugar is one of them. However, other ingredients, such as caffeine in candy and pop, might bother a particular child. And hunger and fatigue can make almost any kid cranky and disruptive.

With less butter than traditional rice crisp cereal squares and with oatmeal and raisins added for fiber and iron, these busy-day snacks are nutritious as well as delicious. Let your kids help by measuring the ingredients.

1 cup	quick-cooking rolled oats	250 mL
1/4 cup	butter	50 mL
1	pkg (250 g) marshmallows (40 regular size)	1
1 tsp	pure vanilla	5 mL
5 cups	rice crisp cereal	1.25 L
1 cup	raisins	250 mL

1 Spread rolled oats on baking sheet; bake in 300°F (150°C) oven for about 10 minutes or until toasted. Lightly grease 13- x 9-inch (3 L) baking dish or spray with nonstick cooking spray; set aside.

2 In large saucepan, melt butter over low heat; add marshmallows and cook, stirring often, until smooth. Remove from heat; stir in vanilla. Working quickly, stir in cereal, toasted oats and raisins until combined. Press into prepared dish. Let cool completely. Cut into squares. *Makes 24 squares.*

Make ahead: Store in airtight container for up to 3 days.

Per square:

calories	107
protein	1 g
total fat	2 g
saturated fat	1 g
cholesterol	5 mg
carbohydrate	21 g
dietary fiber	1 g
sodium	87 mg

R.D.I. Vit A 2%, E 1%, Folate 2%, Ca 1% (7 mg), Iron 8%, Zinc 2%.

Canada's Food Guide Serving:
¼ 🌾 ¼ 🥕

Cranberry Pecan Squares

Dried cranberries add tartness and color to these tasty, easy-to-make squares. They are available in supermarkets.

3/4 cup	firmly packed dried cranberries	175 mL
1/4 cup	cold butter	50 mL
1 cup	all-purpose flour	250 mL
3/4 cup	granulated sugar	175 mL
2 tbsp	1% plain yogurt	25 mL
2	eggs	2
Pinch	salt	Pinch
1/2 cup	coarsely chopped pecans	125 mL

1 In small saucepan, combine cranberries with enough water to cover. Cover and bring to boil; remove from heat and let stand for 1 minute (or microwave*). Drain and let cool. Set aside.

2 In bowl, cut butter into flour until mixture resembles fine crumbs. Stir in 1/4 cup (50 mL) of the sugar and yogurt, mixing well. Press evenly into lightly greased or sprayed 8-inch (2 L) square cake pan. Bake in 350°F (180°C) oven for 15 minutes.

3 Meanwhile, in bowl, beat eggs with remaining 1/2 cup (125 mL) sugar and salt until light; stir in cranberries. Pour over base. Sprinkle pecans evenly over top. Bake in 350°F (180°C) oven for 30 minutes or until set and golden. Let cool slightly in pan; cut into squares. *Makes 18 squares.*

Make ahead: Store in airtight container for up to 5 days or freeze for up to 1 month.

*Cooking Tip

Cranberries are plumped in hot water to make them juicy and tender. This can also be done in the microwave; place in microwaveable dish and add water to cover; microwave on High for 1 minute.

Per square:

calories	125
protein	2 g
total fat	5 g
saturated fat	2 g
cholesterol	31 mg
carbohydrate	18 g
dietary fiber	1 g
sodium	35 mg

R.D.I. Vit A 4%, D 2%, E 2%, C 2%, Folate 2%, Ca 1% (9 mg), Iron 3%, Zinc 4%.

Canada's Food Guide Serving:
¼ 🌾 ¼ 🥕

New-Fangled Hermits

These terrific cookies are a new favorite at our house.
Use any combination of dried fruits (cranberry, cherry, blueberry).

Fiber-Booster

For added fiber in the Hermits, use half whole wheat flour and half all-purpose flour instead of the whole amount of all-purpose flour.

Cooking Tip

If raisins are hard and very dry, plump by pouring boiling water over them and let stand for 10 minutes, then drain well.

2/3 cup	packed brown sugar	150 mL
1/3 cup	butter, softened	75 mL
1	egg	1
1/3 cup	corn syrup	75 mL
1 tsp	each grated orange rind and pure vanilla	5 mL
2 tbsp	fresh orange juice	25 mL
1-3/4 cups	all-purpose flour	425 mL
1/2 tsp	each baking soda and baking powder	2 mL
1/2 tsp	each cinnamon, allspice and nutmeg	2 mL
1/2 cup	each dried blueberries, cranberries, cherries and raisins	125 mL

1 In large bowl, using electric mixer, beat brown sugar with butter until mixed; beat in egg, corn syrup, orange rind, vanilla and orange juice until light and fluffy.

2 In separate bowl, combine flour, baking soda, baking powder, cinnamon, allspice and nutmeg; stir in blueberries, cranberries, cherries and raisins. Stir into butter mixture, mixing well.

3 Drop by rounded tablespoonfuls (15 mL), about 2 inches (5 cm) apart, onto lightly greased baking sheets; flatten tops with back of spoon. Bake in 350°F (180°C) oven for 8 to 10 minutes or until golden. Let stand on baking sheets for 2 to 3 minutes; transfer to racks and let cool completely. *Makes 30 cookies.*

Make ahead: Store in airtight container for up to 1 week or freeze for up to 1 month.

Per cookie:

calories	106
protein	1 g
total fat	2 g
saturated fat	1 g
cholesterol	13 mg
carbohydrate	21 g
dietary fiber	1 g
sodium	52 mg

R.D.I. Vit A 2%, D 1%, E 1%, C 2%, Folate 1%, Ca 1% (13 mg), Iron 4%, Zinc 1%.

Canada's Food Guide Serving:
¼ 🌾 ½ 🥕

Chocolate Banana Cupcakes

Just perfect for a family celebration, these attractive cupcakes make good use of chocolate chips because a few go a long way when studding the tops.

3/4 cup	mashed ripe bananas (2 small)	175 mL
3/4 cup	buttermilk	175 mL
3/4 cup	packed brown sugar	175 mL
1/4 cup	corn syrup	50 mL
3 tbsp	vegetable oil	50 mL
2 tsp	pure vanilla	10 mL
1-3/4 cups	all-purpose flour	425 mL
1/4 cup	unsweetened cocoa powder, sifted	50 mL
1 tsp	baking soda	5 mL
1/2 tsp	salt	2 mL
1/2 cup	chocolate chips	125 mL
1 tbsp	icing sugar	15 mL

1 In bowl, mix bananas, buttermilk, brown sugar, corn syrup, oil and vanilla.

2 Mix together flour, cocoa, baking soda and salt; sprinkle over banana mixture and stir just until moistened.

3 Spray muffin pans with nonstick cooking spray; spoon in batter, filling two-thirds full. Sprinkle chocolate chips over top. Bake in 400°F (200°C) oven for 15 to 20 minutes or until toothpick inserted in center comes out clean. Let cool in pans on rack. Sift icing sugar over top. *Makes 12 cupcakes.*

Make ahead: Store in airtight container for up to 2 days.

To Sift or Not To Sift

- When a recipe calls for sifting, use a sifter specially designed for baking or a fine-mesh sieve.
- All-purpose flour does not require sifting.
- Sift cocoa powder and icing sugar to eliminate any lumps.
- If "sifted" is written before the ingredient, you sift before you measure; if "sifted" is written after the ingredient (i.e, 1/4 cup/ 50 mL cocoa powder, sifted), you measure then sift.

Per cupcake:

calories	232
protein	3 g
total fat	6 g
saturated fat	2 g
cholesterol	1 mg
carbohydrate	43 g
dietary fiber	2 g
sodium	221 mg

R.D.I. Vit E 8%, C 2%, Folate 3%, Ca 4% (39 mg), Iron 12%, Zinc 5%.

Canada's Food Guide Serving:
¾

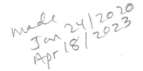
made Jan 24/2020
Apr 18/2023

Lemon Blueberry Coffee Cake

Serve this terrific cake anytime — for breakfast, brunch, dessert,
with coffee or just as a snack.

1-1/2 cups	all-purpose flour	375 mL
1-1/2 tsp	baking powder	7 mL
1 tsp	baking soda	5 mL
1/2 tsp	salt	2 mL
	Grated rind from 2 medium lemons	
1/4 cup	butter	50 mL
3/4 cup	granulated sugar	175 mL
2	eggs, lightly beaten	2
1 tsp	vanilla	5 mL
1 cup	plain 1% yogurt or buttermilk	250 mL
1 cup	blueberries, fresh or frozen (not thawed)	250 mL
Topping:		
1/4 cup	packed brown sugar	50 mL
2 tsp	cinnamon	10 mL

1 Spray 8 x 8 inch (2 L) cake pan with nonstick cooking spray. In bowl, stir together flour, baking powder, baking soda, salt and lemon rind.

2 In large bowl, cream butter; beat in sugar until light. Beat in eggs one at a time, then add vanilla. Alternately add flour mixture and yogurt to butter mixture, making 3 additions of flour and 2 of yogurt. Spread half in pan. Sprinkle with blueberries. Gently spread remaining batter over top.

3 Topping: In small bowl, mix sugar with cinnamon. Sprinkle over batter. Bake in 350°F (180°C) oven for 45 to 55 minutes or until cake tester inserted in center comes out clean. Let cool in pan on rack for 10 minutes. Remove from pan and let cool on rack. Makes 12 servings. (in Bundt pan, reduce to 35-40 min)

Make ahead: Wrap and refrigerate for up to 2 days or freeze for up to 1 month.

Per serving:

calories	205
protein	5 g
total fat	6 g
saturated fat	1 g
cholesterol	29 mg
carbohydrate	39 g
dietary fiber	1 g
sodium	230 mg

R.D.I. Vit A 3%, D 12%, E 6%, C 7%, Folate 4%, Ca 9% (104 mg), Iron 9%, Zinc 5%.

Canada's Food Guide Serving:

1

Chocolate Chip Coffee Cake

*Chocolate chips and toasted pecans add a richness and crunch
to this easy-to-make cake.*

1/4 cup	coarsely chopped pecans	50 mL
1 cup	chocolate chips (6 oz/175 g)	250 mL
1/4 cup	packed brown sugar	50 mL
2 tsp	cinnamon	10 mL
Cake:		
1/4 cup	butter	25 mL
3/4 cup	granulated sugar	175 mL
2	eggs	2
2 tsp	pure vanilla	10 mL
1-3/4 cups	all-purpose flour	425 mL
2 tsp	baking powder	10 mL
1 tsp	baking soda	5 mL
1/4 tsp	salt	1 mL
1 cup	1% plain yogurt	250 mL

1 Toast pecans on baking sheet in 350°F (180°C) oven for 5 minutes or until golden; let cool. In bowl, mix chocolate chips, pecans, brown sugar and cinnamon.

2 Cake: In large bowl, cream butter until fluffy; add sugar and beat until well mixed; beat in eggs one at a time, then add vanilla. In separate bowl, combine flour, baking powder, baking soda and salt. Alternately add flour mixture and yogurt to creamed butter mixture, making 3 additions of flour and 2 of yogurt.

3 Lightly grease or spray 10-inch (3 L) Bundt pan with nonstick cooking spray. Spoon in half of the batter; sprinkle with half of the nut mixture. Spread with remaining batter; sprinkle with remaining nut mixture, lightly pressing into batter.

4 Bake in 350°F (180°C) oven for 45 to 60 minutes or until cake tester inserted in center comes out clean. Let cool in pan on rack. Turn out onto serving plate, chocolate and nuts facing up. *Makes 12 servings.*

Make ahead: Cover and store for up to 1 day.

Cooking Tip

Make the most of the fat you use. Here, a minimum of oil is used; the fat in the nuts and chocolate chips adds flavor and texture as well as richness. Evaporated milk adds creaminess with much less fat than cream.

Per serving:

calories	276
protein	5 g
total fat	9 g
saturated fat	3 g
cholesterol	19 mg
carbohydrate	45 g
dietary fiber	2 g
sodium	242 mg

R.D.I. Vit A 2%, D 9%, E 6%, C 3%, Folate 4%, Ca 10% (106 mg), Iron 12%, Zinc 8%.

Canada's Food Guide Serving:
1 🌾

Dessert

Lemon Cake with Lemon Cream or Raspberry Sauce

Apple Cranberry Streusel Cake

Easy Chocolate Cake with Chocolate Buttermilk Icing

Cantaloupe and Blueberries with Fresh Strawberry Sauce

Citrus Frozen Yogurt with Mango

Apple Berry Crisp

Strawberry Apple Cobbler

Apricot Raspberry Parfait

Ginger Citrus Fruit Salad

Orange Mousse

Deep-Dish Apple Apricot Phyllo Pie

Easy, No-Roll Food Processor Pastry

Peach Blueberry Pie

Lemon Chocolate Tart

Strawberries with Lemon Cream in Phyllo Pastry Cups

French Lemon Tart

Lemon Cheesecake with Raspberry Glaze

Cranberry Yogurt Flan

Black Forest Frozen Yogurt Cake or Pie

Orange Mousse Meringue Pie

Nutrition Notes

Lactose Intolerance: "Can't Tolerate Milk?"

Diabetes: "An Update on Diabetes"

Irritable Bowels: "Dietary Help for Irritable Bowels"

Lemon Cake with Lemon Cream or Raspberry Sauce

The recipe for this great-tasting cake comes from my friend
and recipe tester Shannon Graham. Serve it with Lemon Cream (opposite page)
or Raspberry Sauce (opposite page) or with ice cream or fresh fruit.

Whey

The whey or drained liquid from yogurt contains B vitamins and minerals and is low in fat. Refrigerate it and use it in soups.

Kitchen Tip

To measure the size of a cake pan or Bundt pan, measure across the top.

1/2 cup	butter or soft margarine	125 mL
2 cups	granulated sugar	500 mL
2	eggs	2
1/4 cup	1% or 2% plain yogurt	50 mL
	Grated rind of 2 large lemons	
3 cups	all-purpose flour	750 mL
2 tsp	baking powder	10 mL
1 cup	1% milk	250 mL
Glaze:		
2/3 cup	fresh lemon juice	150 mL
1/2 cup	granulated sugar	125 mL

1 In large bowl, using electric mixer, beat butter with sugar until light and fluffy; beat in eggs, yogurt and lemon rind. Mix flour with baking powder; beat into egg mixture alternately with milk, making three additions of flour mixture and two of milk.

2 Spoon into greased and floured 10-inch (3 L) Bundt pan. Bake in 350°F (180°C) oven for 50 minutes or until cake tester inserted in center comes out clean. Let stand in pan on rack for 5 minutes.

3 Glaze: Stir lemon juice with sugar until sugar is dissolved. Invert cake onto rimmed plate; using toothpick, poke 1-inch (2.5 cm) deep holes in top of cake. Brush glaze over cake. Let cool. *Makes 16 servings.*

Make ahead: Cover and store for up to 2 days.

Per serving (no sauce):

calories	278
protein	4 g
total fat	7 g
saturated fat	4 g
cholesterol	43 mg
carbohydrate	51 g
dietary fiber	1 g
sodium	110 mg

R.D.I. Vit A 7%, D 5%, E 2%, C 8%, Folate 4%, Ca 5% (50 mg), Iron 8%, Zinc 4%.

Canada's Food Guide Serving:
1 🌾

Lemon Cream

This creamy sauce is perfect with cake, fresh fruit or pie.

1 cup	extra-thick (Greek-style) or drained plain yogurt*	250 mL
1/3 cup	granulated sugar	75 mL
	Grated rind of 1 medium lemon	
1 tbsp	fresh lemon juice	15 mL

1 In small bowl, combine yogurt, sugar, lemon rind and juice, stirring well. Cover and refrigerate for 30 minutes or for up to 3 days. *Makes about 1-1/4 cups (300 mL).*

Make ahead: Cover and refrigerate for up to 3 days or to "best before" date on yogurt container.

*For information on draining yogurt, see page 22.

Per 2 tbsp:	
calories	**49**
protein	**2 g**
total fat	**trace**
saturated fat	trace
cholesterol	**2 mg**
carbohydrate	**9 g**
sodium	**21 mg**

R.D.I. Vit C 3%, Folate 2%, Ca 7% (76 mg), Zinc 4%.

Raspberry Sauce

Serve with Lemon Cake (page 260), Easy Chocolate Cake (page 264), frozen yogurt or fresh fruit.

2	pkg (300 g each) frozen unsweetened raspberries	2
1/4 cup	granulated sugar	50 mL

1 Thaw raspberries; drain and reserve 1/2 cup (125 mL) juice. Press berries through sieve over bowl to remove seeds. Stir in enough of the reserved juice to make sauce consistency. Stir in sugar. *Makes about 2 cups (500 mL).*

Make ahead: Cover and refrigerate for up to 5 days.

Per 1/4 cup (50 mL):	
calories	**44**
protein	**1 g**
total fat	**0 g**
cholesterol	**0 mg**
carbohydrate	**10 g**
sodium	**0 mg**

R.D.I. Vit A 1%, E 3%, C 25%, Folate 7%, Ca 1% (13 mg), Iron 2%, Zinc 3%.

Canada's Food Guide Serving:

1 🥕

Can't Tolerate Milk?

Don't pass on a recipe just because it has milk in it! You'd be missing out on both taste and nutrition.

If you are one of those people who can't handle milk and milk products without suffering from stomach cramps, bloating, gas and diarrhea, you may have a shortage of lactase enzymes necessary to digest the lactose sugar. Left undigested, lactose sugar ferments in the gastrointestinal tract and causes the unpleasant symptoms. The degree of lactose intolerance varies from person to person, from mild to severe. Sometimes it is only a temporary condition that develops after a bout of severe diarrhea.

Research shows that even people with severe lactose intolerance can tolerate up to 1 cup (250 mL) of milk with a meal. So try using small amounts of milk throughout the day.

HEALTHY EATING TIPS: Lactose Intolerance
- Try lactose-reduced milk (found in the milk section of most grocery stores). It's 99% lactose free. Or use liquid lactase drops (found in drugstores) to make lactose-reduced milk at home.
- Take lactase enzyme tablets (also found in drugstores) at meals containing regular milk or milk products. These tablets take the worry out of dining away from home.
- Try small servings of aged cheeses such as Cheddar, Swiss, brick, camembert, limburger and Parmesan. These cheeses contain very little lactose.
- Eat yogurt. The bacteria in yogurt produce lactase enzyme, which continues to digest lactose even after the yogurt is eaten.
- If you are severely intolerant, drink a plant-based beverage such as a soy or rice beverage in place of milk. Look for a product that is enriched with vitamins A, D, B12, riboflavin, calcium and zinc.

Apple Cranberry Streusel Cake

Serve this golden apple-topped cake with coffee for brunch or dessert.
If you are using frozen cranberries, don't thaw them first.

1/3 cup	butter or margarine, softened	75 mL
3/4 cup	granulated sugar	175 mL
2	eggs	2
1-1/2 cups	all-purpose flour	375 mL
1 tsp	baking powder	5 mL
1/2 tsp	baking soda	2 mL
	Grated rind from 1 medium lemon	
2/3 cup	2% plain yogurt	150 mL
1 cup	cranberries (fresh, frozen or dried)	250 mL
2	apples, peeled and thinly sliced	2
Streusel:		
1/2 cup	packed brown sugar	125 mL
1-1/2 tsp	cinnamon	7 mL

1 In large bowl, using electric mixer, beat butter with sugar until light and fluffy; beat in eggs, one at a time, beating well after each addition.

2 Mix flour, baking powder, baking soda and lemon rind; beat into egg mixture alternately with yogurt, making three additions of flour mixture and two of yogurt.

3 Spread half of the batter into greased and floured 10-inch (3 L) springform pan. Arrange cranberries over top.

4 Streusel: Combine brown sugar with cinnamon; sprinkle half over cranberries. Spread remaining batter over top; arrange apple slices in slightly overlapping circles over top. Sprinkle with remaining sugar mixture.

5 Bake in 350°F (180°C) oven for 50 to 60 minutes or until golden and toothpick inserted in center comes out clean. Let cool on rack for 20 minutes before removing side of pan. *Makes 12 servings.*

Make ahead: Cover and refrigerate for up to 1 day.

Lower-Fat Tip

Choose a soft-tub non-hydrogenated margarine instead of butter most of the time because margarine is lower in saturated fat. However, both butter and margarine contain the same amount of fat and the same number of calories.

Per serving:

calories	222
protein	3 g
total fat	6 g
saturated fat	4 g
cholesterol	50 mg
carbohydrate	39 g
dietary fiber	1 g
sodium	147 mg

R.D.I. Vit A 7%, D 3%, E 2%, C 3%, Folate 3%, Ca 5% (55 mg), Iron 8%, Zinc 4%.

Canada's Food Guide Serving:
¾ 🌾 ¼ 🥕

Easy Chocolate Cake with Chocolate Buttermilk Icing

This dense, rich chocolate cake has all the taste and about half the fat of a regular chocolate cake. For the most intense chocolate flavor, use Dutch process unsweetened cocoa powder. Domestic brands are available in supermarkets.

Cooking Tip

Adding coffee to chocolate dishes enhances the chocolate flavor.

2 tbsp	espresso powder or instant coffee granules	25 mL
1/2 cup	boiling water	125 mL
2-1/4 cups	all-purpose flour	550 mL
2 cups	granulated sugar	500 mL
3/4 cup	unsweetened cocoa powder, sifted	175 mL
1-1/2 tsp	each baking powder and baking soda	7 mL
1 tsp	salt	5 mL
1-3/4 cups	buttermilk	425 mL
2	eggs, beaten	2
1/4 cup	vegetable oil	50 mL
2 tsp	vanilla	10 mL
	Chocolate Buttermilk Icing (page 266)	

1 Dissolve espresso powder in boiling water; let cool. Grease or spray 13- x 9-inch (3 L) baking dish with nonstick cooking spray; line bottom with waxed paper.

2 In large bowl, mix flour, sugar, cocoa, baking powder, baking soda and salt. Beat in buttermilk, eggs, oil, vanilla and espresso mixture; beat at medium speed for 2 minutes.

3 Pour into prepared pan. Bake in 350°F (180°C) oven for 40 to 45 minutes or until top springs back when lightly touched. Let cool in pan on rack for 20 minutes. Remove from pan; let cool completely on rack. Spread with chocolate icing. *Makes 16 servings.*

Make ahead: Cover and store for up to 2 days.

Per serving (with icing):

calories	258
protein	5 g
total fat	5 g
saturated fat	1 g
cholesterol	28 mg
carbohydrate	51 g
dietary fiber	3 g
sodium	324 mg

R.D.I. Vit A 1%, D 2%, E 8%, Folate 4%, Ca 6% (66 mg), Iron 14%, Zinc 9%.

Canada's Food Guide Serving: ¾ 🌾

Chocolate Buttermilk Icing

Cooking Tip

For a thicker icing, stir in enough sifted icing sugar to reach desired thickness.

1/2 cup	granulated sugar	125 mL
1/2 cup	unsweetened cocoa powder, sifted	125 mL
1/2 cup	buttermilk	125 mL
1/2 tsp	vanilla	2 mL

I In small heavy saucepan, mix sugar with cocoa; whisk in buttermilk until smooth. Stirring constantly, cook over medium heat until simmering; cook, stirring constantly, for 2 minutes. Remove from heat; stir in vanilla. Let cool for 2 hours. (Icing will thicken upon cooling.) *Makes 1 cup (250 mL).*

Make ahead: Place plastic wrap directly on surface; store for up to 5 days.

Per 4 tsp (20 mL):

calories	**45**
protein	**I g**
total fat	**I g**
saturated fat	**trace**
cholesterol	**0 mg**
carbohydrate	**II g**
dietary fiber	**I g**
sodium	**II mg**

R.D.I. Folate 1%, Ca 1% (16 mg), Iron 4%, Zinc 3%.

KITCHEN TIPS

Measuring Ingredients

- Use a measuring cup with a spout for measuring liquids. Place on a level surface and check at eye level.
- Use metal or plastic measuring cups for measuring dry ingredients. Spoon dry ingredients such as flour into cup, then level off with the flat side of a knife. Avoid shaking or tapping measure to level.
- Pack butter or margarine firmly.
- Use the correct pan size. To check the pan size for traditional cake pans and pie plates (or dishes), turn pan over and measure across the bottom.
- To determine the volume measure of your dish, fill it with water then measure the water. For example, if your cake pan holds approximately 8 cups/2000 mL (2000 mL = 2 L), it will be suitable for a recipe calling for a 2 L cake pan.

Lining and Greasing Pans

- Spray pans with a nonstick cooking spray or brush lightly with vegetable oil.
- When a recipe calls for lining the bottom of a pan, use parchment or waxed paper. Lining the sides of a pan isn't usually necessary unless called for in the recipe to keep the edges of a cake from drying out or to protect the ingredients from discoloration.

Beating Egg Whites

- Start with eggs at room temperature. If you don't have time to let them stand, cover them with warm water for a few minutes.
- Use a glass or metal (not plastic) mixing bowl and clean beaters.
- Make sure there is no yolk in the whites.
- To beat egg whites, beat with electric mixer or whisk until stiff and glossy. Do not overbeat because the egg whites will get lumpy and begin to lose volume.

An Update on Diabetes

People who worry about what to serve a guest who has diabetes may be operating under some outdated views. The diet for diabetes has done a complete turnabout in the last decade or so. What's appropriate for people with diabetes is simply the same healthy eating pattern as outlined on page 1.

A Diabetes Review

People with diabetes lack or are resistant to the hormone insulin and therefore can't properly utilize glucose, the main energy source for every cell in the body. The primary goal in the treatment of diabetes is to control the fluctuations in blood sugar levels so as to improve the person's feelings of well-being and to reduce the longer-term health risks.

HEALTHY EATING TIPS: Feeding a Guest with Diabetes

- People with diabetes can eat according to the same healthy eating pattern (see page 1) as everyone else. No special foods are required.
- Meal regularity and timing are important, especially for those who take insulin. Ask your guest what time is best to serve meals.
- If for some reason a meal can't be served at the required time, make sure a snack — such as low-fat cheese and crackers — is available.
- Keep meals low in fat. Offer lower-fat choices — milk for coffee instead of cream, light salad dressings, vegetables with a lemon wedge not butter.
- Meals should contain complex carbohydrates or starchy foods — pasta, rice, couscous, bread or any legume dish.
- Sugar is allowed when it's part of a total meal. Try the Ginger Citrus Fruit Salad (page 274) or the Apricot Raspberry Parfait (page 273).
- Offer lots of vegetables with dinner.
- Use salt moderately.
- Have a non-alcoholic beverage choice available such as soda or mineral water or a sugar-free soft drink.
- At breakfast, offer whole grain cereal, 1% milk, low-fat yogurt, low-fat whole grain muffins, peanut butter, a poached egg, and fruit such as an orange or grapefruit.

Two Types of Diabetes

- Type 2, the most common type, is associated with being over-weight and physically inactive. Type 2 is treated mainly through healthy diet and exercise, although an oral medication may also be taken to stimulate the pancreas to produce more insulin.
- Type 1 is a disease of the pancreas and less common than Type 2. Healthy eating, exercise and daily injections of insulin are important aspects of treatment.

Cantaloupe and Blueberries with Fresh Strawberry Sauce

This is a lovely, refreshing summer dessert. Serve with Double-Chocolate Cookies (page 251) or New-Fangled Hermits (page 254).

2 cups	sliced fresh strawberries	500 mL
2 tbsp	granulated sugar	25 mL
2 tbsp	kirsch (optional)	25 mL
1 tbsp	fresh lemon juice	15 mL
1	cantaloupe	1
1 cup	blueberries	250 mL

1 In blender or food processor, purée strawberries. Add sugar, kirsch (if using) and lemon juice; process to mix.

2 Halve cantaloupe; scoop out seeds. Cut flesh into bite-size pieces. Spoon cantaloupe and blueberries into 4 stemmed glasses.

3 Drizzle sauce over fruit. *Makes 4 servings.*

Make ahead: Through step 2, cover and refrigerate for up to 6 hours. Remove from refrigerator 30 minutes before serving.

Brunch Menu

Mushroom Bruschetta (page 23)
Salmon and Spinach Strata (page 221) or
Asparagus and Mushroom Gratin (page 224)
Spinach Salad with Walnut Vinaigrette (page 38)
Cantaloupe and Blueberries with Fresh Strawberry Sauce (this page) or
Apple Berry Crisp (page 271)

Serving Tip

Garnish each serving with a strawberry fan. They are easy to make; just slice strawberry from tip almost but not completely through, then fan out slices.

Nutrition Tip

Cantaloupe is an excellent source of the antioxidants vitamin C and beta carotene. When cantaloupe is teamed with strawberries (also an excellent source of vitamin C), as it is here, one serving will provide more than 175 percent of your daily requirement of vitamin C and 43 percent of beta carotene (Vitamin A).

Per serving:

calories	114
protein	2 g
total fat	1 g
cholesterol	0 mg
carbohydrate	28 g
dietary fiber	4 g
sodium	16 mg

R.D.I. Vit A 43%, E 7%, C 173%, Folate 18%, Ca 3% (28 mg), Iron 5%, Zinc 4%.

Canada's Food Guide Serving:
3

Citrus Frozen Yogurt with Mango

I had this dynamic dessert at a dinner party hosted by Monda Rosenberg, Chatelaine magazine's food editor. It was so wonderful that I immediately asked her for the recipe. The grated lemon and lime rind give the yogurt a fabulous fresh fruity flavor. It would also be lovely with fresh berries or peaches — in fact, any fresh fruit in season.

8 cups	frozen vanilla yogurt	2 L
2	lemons	2
2	limes	2
3	large ripe mangoes, peeled and sliced	3
	Fresh mint leaves	

1 Let yogurt stand at room temperature just until it can be stirred, 15 to 30 minutes.

2 Finely grate rind from lemons and limes. Squeeze 1 tbsp (15 mL) each of the lime and lemon juice; set aside.

3 Turn softened yogurt into large bowl. Stir in rinds and juices until mixed. Spoon back into yogurt container; cover and freeze until hard, about 1 hour.

4 Arrange scoops of frozen yogurt on dessert plates. Attractively surround with mangoes; garnish with fresh mint. *Makes 12 servings.*

Make ahead: Through step 3 for up to 1 month.

Per serving:

calories	**247**
protein	**6 g**
total fat	**7 g**
saturated fat	5 g
cholesterol	13 mg
carbohydrate	**42 g**
dietary fiber	**2 g**
sodium	**78 mg**

R.D.I. Vit A 28%, E 7%, C 37%, Folate 5%, Ca 18% (194 mg), Iron 1%, Zinc 7%.

Canada's Food Guide Serving:
½ ▮ ½ 🥕

Apple Berry Crisp

Caramba, one of my favorite restaurants in Whistler, B.C., has a fabulous berry crisp, packed with blackberries and raspberries. Here's my version to make anytime of year. Use any combination of frozen or fresh berries.

3/4 cup	granulated sugar	175 mL
1/4 cup	all-purpose flour	50 mL
	Grated rind of 1 lemon	
4 cups	sliced peeled apples (about 4)	1 L
1	pkg (300 g) frozen blueberries (2 cups/500 mL)	1
1	pkg (300 g) unsweetened frozen raspberries (2 cups/500 mL)	1
2 cups	fresh or frozen cranberries	500 mL
Topping:		
1-1/2 cups	quick-cooking rolled oats	375 mL
3/4 cup	packed brown sugar	175 mL
1/4 cup	whole wheat flour	50 mL
2 tsp	cinnamon	10 mL
1/4 cup	butter or soft margarine, melted	50 mL

1 In large bowl, stir together sugar, flour and lemon rind. Add apples, blueberries, raspberries and cranberries; stir gently to mix. Spoon into 13- x 9-inch (3 L) baking dish.

2 Topping: In small bowl, stir together oats, sugar, flour and cinnamon; drizzle with butter and toss to mix. Spoon over fruit. Bake in 375°F (190°C) oven for 40 to 50 minutes or until bubbling and topping is golden. Serve warm or at room temperature. *Makes 8 servings.*

Make ahead. Let stand for up to 6 hours; serve at room temperature or reheat.

Serving Tip

Serve with frozen vanilla yogurt or extra-thick plain yogurt mixed with grated lemon rind and sweetened to taste with sugar.

Fat-lowering Tip

Keep washed fresh fruit and canned fruit cups handy for instant, low-fat snacks.

Per serving:	
calories	368
protein	4 g
total fat	8 g
saturated fat	4 g
cholesterol	16 mg
carbohydrate	75 g
dietary fiber	8 g
sodium	68 mg

R.D.I. Vit A 6%, E 8%, C 20%, Folate 5%, Ca 5% (52 mg), Iron 14%, Zinc 10%.

Canada's Food Guide Serving:

¾ 🌾   2 🥕

Strawberry Apple Cobbler

You can make this well-liked dessert any time of year with fresh or frozen strawberries.

Strawberry Rhubarb Cobbler

Increase sugar to 3/4 cup (175 mL); substitute 4 cups (1 L) coarsely chopped (3/4-inch/2 cm pieces) rhubarb for the apples; reduce strawberries to 3 cups (750 mL). If using frozen rhubarb, thaw first.

Nutrition Tip

Strawberries are an excellent source of vitamin C and high in fiber.

1/2 cup	granulated sugar	125 mL
3 tbsp	all-purpose flour	50 mL
1 tsp	cinnamon	5 mL
	Grated rind of 1 medium lemon	
5 cups	fresh strawberries or 2 pkg (300 g each) frozen unsweetened (not thawed)	1.25 L
2 cups	coarsely chopped peeled apples	500 mL
2 tbsp	fresh lemon juice	25 mL
Topping:		
1 cup	all-purpose flour	250 mL
3 tbsp	granulated sugar	50 mL
1 tsp	baking powder	5 mL
1/4 tsp	each baking soda and salt	1 mL
3 tbsp	cold butter, cut in bits	50 mL
2/3 cup	buttermilk	150 mL

1 In bowl, mix sugar, flour, cinnamon and lemon rind; stir in strawberries, apples then lemon juice. Spread in 8-cup (2 L) shallow baking dish; bake in 400°F (200°C) oven for 10 minutes.

2 Topping: In bowl, mix flour, sugar, baking powder, baking soda and salt. Using fingers or two knives, cut in butter until crumbly.

3 With fork, stir in buttermilk until soft dough forms. Drop by spoonfuls onto fruit in 6 evenly spaced mounds. Bake for 30 to 40 minutes or until top is golden and undersides of biscuits are cooked. *Makes 6 servings.*

Make ahead: Through step 2; let stand for 2 hours. Or through step 3 for up to 4 hours; serve at room temperature or reheat.

Per serving:

calories	**302**
protein	**4 g**
total fat	**7 g**
saturated fat	4 g
cholesterol	17 mg
carbohydrate	**58 g**
dietary fiber	**4 g**
sodium	**277 mg**

R.D.I. Vit A 6%, E 3%, C 90%, Folate 8%, Ca 7% (81 mg), Iron 12%, Zinc 5%.

Canada's Food Guide Serving:

1¼ 🌾 2 🥕

Apricot Raspberry Parfait

*This delicious, creamy, low-fat dessert looks pretty garnished with
fresh raspberries and mint leaves.*

1	can (14 oz/398 mL) apricots (undrained)*	1
1/4 cup	granulated sugar	50 mL
1	pkg (7 g) unflavored gelatin	1
1 cup	1% or 2% plain yogurt	250 mL
2 tbsp	fresh lemon juice	25 mL
1/4 tsp	almond extract	1 mL
1	pkg (300 g) frozen unsweetened raspberries, thawed, or 2 cups (500 mL) fresh**	1

1 Drain apricots, pouring 1/4 cup (50 mL) of the juice into saucepan or microwaveable
dish; stir in 3 tbsp (45 mL) of the sugar. Sprinkle gelatin over top; let stand for
5 minutes to soften. Cook over low heat or microwave at Medium (50% power) for
40 seconds or until gelatin is dissolved.

2 In food processor or blender, purée apricots. In bowl, stir apricot purée, yogurt,
gelatin mixture, lemon juice and almond extract until smooth.

3 Press raspberries and juice through sieve over bowl; stir in remaining sugar. Reserve
1/4 cup (50 mL) of the raspberry purée for garnish. Stir remaining raspberry purée
into apricot mixture. Spoon into four parfait or stemmed glasses. Cover and
refrigerate for 1-1/2 hours or until set. Spoon reserved raspberry purée over top.
Makes 4 servings.

Make ahead: Cover and refrigerate for up to 2 days.

* Substitution Tip
To use dried apricots
instead of canned, cover
and simmer 12 whole dried
apricots (1/2 cup/125 mL)
in 1/2 cup (125 mL) water
for 20 minutes or until very
tender. Purée with any
liquid until smooth. Soften
gelatin in 1/4 cup (50 mL)
cold water.

** Substitution Tip
Raspberries add extra flavor
and color. However, you can
omit them and add another
1 cup (250 mL) yogurt.

Per serving:

calories	162
protein	6 g
total fat	1 g
saturated fat	trace
cholesterol	2 mg
carbohydrate	34 g
dietary fiber	1 g
sodium	53 mg

R.D.I. Vit A 19%, E 12%, C 37%,
Folate 11%, Ca 12% (135 mg), Iron 5%,
Zinc 10%.

Canada's Food Guide Serving:
1¾ ¼

Orange Mousse

Creamy and smooth, this sophisticated dessert is truly easy to make.
Garnish with fresh berries, orange sections or candied orange rind.

Lower-Fat Cooking

For a fat-restricted diet, substitute 1/2 cup (125 mL) plain yogurt for the whipping cream and increase sugar to 1/2 cup (125 mL). Calories will be reduced to 119 and fat to 1 gram per serving.

Lower-Sugar Cooking

For people with diabetes, substitute 1/3 cup (75 mL) Splenda for the sugar.

1	pkg (7 g) gelatin	1
2/3 cup	fresh orange juice	150 mL
1 cup	1% or 2% plain yogurt	250 mL
1/3 cup	granulated sugar	75 mL
2 tbsp	orange liqueur (optional)	25 mL
	Finely grated rind of 1 medium orange	
1/2 cup	whipping cream, lightly whipped	125 mL

1 In bowl or saucepan, sprinkle gelatin over orange juice; let stand for 5 minutes. Microwave at Medium-High (70% power) for 1 minute, or stir over medium-low heat for 1 minute, or until dissolved.

2 Stir in yogurt, sugar, liqueur (if using) and orange rind. Fold in whipped cream. Spoon into individual dishes or stemmed glasses. Refrigerate until set, about 1-1/2 hours. *Makes 6 servings.*

Make ahead: Cover and refrigerate for up to 1 day.

Per serving:

calories	152
protein	4 g
total fat	7 g
saturated fat	5 g
cholesterol	27 mg
carbohydrate	18 g
dietary fiber	1 g
sodium	39 mg

R.D.I. Vit A 9%, E 2%, C 27%, Folate 5%, Ca 9% (95 mg), Iron 1%, Zinc 4%.

Canada's Food Guide Serving:
¼

Deep-Dish Apple Apricot Phyllo Pie

Sweet apricots and tart lemon add a novel twist of flavor to this apple pie.
Using a minimum of butter between the phyllo layers makes this pie lower in fat than one
with a regular pastry crust.

9 cups	sliced peeled apples	2.25 L
3/4 cup	dried apricots, cut in strips	175 mL
	Grated rind of 1 lemon	
2 tbsp	fresh lemon juice	25 mL
1/2 cup	granulated sugar	125 mL
2 tbsp	all-purpose flour	25 mL
1-1/2 tsp	cinnamon	7 mL
Pinch	ground nutmeg	Pinch
1 cup	coarse fresh bread crumbs	250 mL
Phyllo Topping:		
1 tbsp	granulated sugar	15 mL
1/4 tsp	cinnamon	1 mL
4	sheets phyllo pastry	4
4 tsp	butter, melted	20 mL

1 In large bowl, combine apples, apricots, lemon rind and juice. Mix together sugar, flour, cinnamon and nutmeg; stir into apple mixture. Spoon into 13- x 9-inch (3 L) shallow baking dish. Sprinkle bread crumbs over top.

2 Phyllo Topping: Mix sugar with cinnamon. Lay one sheet of phyllo on work surface, keeping remainder covered to prevent drying out. Brush lightly with butter; sprinkle with one-quarter of the cinnamon mixture. Lay second sheet on top; brush with butter and sprinkle with another quarter of the cinnamon mixture. Repeat layers twice.

3 Trim 1-inch (2.5 cm) border from phyllo. Place phyllo on top of fruit; roll edges under and press into sides of pan. Using serrated knife, cut slits in top of pastry; score into 8 portions. Bake in 350°F (180°C) oven for 50 minutes or until golden brown and apples are tender. *Makes 8 servings.*

Make ahead: Can stand for up to 6 hours; reheat for 15 minutes to crisp pastry.

Per serving:

calories	**231**
protein	**2 g**
total fat	**3 g**
saturated fat	1 g
cholesterol	5 mg
carbohydrate	**51 g**
dietary fiber	**5 g**
sodium	**109 mg**

R.D.I. Vit A 10%, E 4%, C 12%,
Folate 2%, Ca 2% (25 mg), Iron 11%,
Zinc 3%.

Canada's Food Guide Serving:
½ 🌾   2 🥕

Easy, No-Roll Food Processor Pastry

This is as easy to make and similar in method as a graham cracker or cookie crust pastry. I prefer a pastry made with butter rather than with oil (even though butter is higher in saturated fat), because it is more tender and I prefer the flavor. I keep the butter to a minimum and make a single-crust pie.

Baked Pie Shell

To bake an unfilled pie shell, prick pastry with fork (to prevent shrinking or puffing up). Line with foil; cover foil with dried beans or pie weights. Bake in 375°F (190°C) oven for 20 minutes; remove foil and beans. Prick shell if puffed; bake for 5 to 10 minutes longer or until golden brown.

1-1/4 cups	all-purpose flour	300 mL
1/4 cup	cold butter, cut in chunks	50 mL
2 tbsp	granulated sugar	25 mL
2 tbsp	cold water	25 mL
2 tsp	white vinegar	10 mL

1 In food processor, combine flour, butter and sugar; process using on/off turns until mixture resembles coarse crumbs. Add water and vinegar; process using on/off turns until mixture barely starts to hold together. (If you press a little of the mixture between fingers, it sticks together.)

2 Turn into 9-inch (23 cm) pie plate or flan pan; using hands or back of large spoon, spread evenly over bottom and up side of plate, pressing firmly so mixture holds together (similar to graham cracker crust). Refrigerate for 15 minutes.
Makes one 9-inch (23 cm) pie shell, or 8 servings.

Make ahead: Cover and refrigerate for up to 1 day.

Per 1/8 shell:

calories	134
protein	2 g
total fat	6 g
saturated fat	4 g
cholesterol	16 mg
carbohydrate	18 g
dietary fiber	1 g
sodium	59 mg

R.D.I. Vit A 5%, E 1%, Folate 2%, Ca 0% (5 mg), Iron 6%, Zinc 2%.

Canada's Food Guide Serving:
1 🌾

Peach Blueberry Pie

Juicy ripe peaches and blueberries, sparked with lemon, make a fabulous summer pie.

1/2 cup	granulated sugar	125 mL
1/4 cup	all-purpose flour	50 mL
1 tsp	cinnamon	5 mL
	Grated rind of 1 medium lemon	
5 cups	thickly sliced peeled peaches	1.25 L
1 cup	blueberries	250 mL
1 tbsp	fresh lemon juice	15 mL
1	unbaked 9-inch (23 cm) pie shell (see Easy, No-Roll Food Processor Pastry, opposite page)	1
Topping:		
1	large peach, peeled and thinly sliced	1
2 tsp	fresh lemon juice	10 mL

1 In bowl, stir together sugar, flour, cinnamon and lemon rind. Add peaches, blueberries and lemon juice; stir to mix. Spoon evenly into pie shell.

2 Bake in 400°F (200°C) oven for 50 minutes or until bubbling and peaches are fork-tender. (If top browns too quickly, cover loosely with foil.) Let stand for at least 30 minutes or for up to 8 hours.

3 Topping: Brush peach slices with lemon juice; arrange over pie. *Makes 8 servings.*

Peach Raspberry Pie: Substitute 1 cup (250 mL) raspberries for blueberries.

Plum Tart: Substitute 5 cups (1.25 L) sliced pitted ripe plums (any kind) for the peaches and blueberries; omit lemon juice; increase sugar to 1 cup (250 mL).

Nectarine and Plum Tart: Substitute 2-1/2 cups (625 mL) each sliced nectarines and plums (any kind of ripe plum) for peaches and blueberries. Just before serving, sprinkle with icing sugar.

Peach Cream Pie: Omit blueberries. Mix 1 cup (250 mL) light 5% sour cream and 1 egg, lightly beaten, with sugar mixture.

Cooking Tip

To peel peaches: Some peaches are so ripe, the skin peels off very easily. If not, immerse peaches in a bowl of boiling water for 1 minute before peeling. To prevent peaches from darkening, rub whole peeled peach with cut lemon or sprinkle lemon juice over sliced peaches.

Per serving:

calories	263
protein	4 g
total fat	6 g
saturated fat	4 g
cholesterol	16 mg
carbohydrate	51 g
dietary fiber	3 g
sodium	61 mg

R.D.I. Vit A 11%, E 11%, C 17%, Folate 4%, Ca 2% (17 mg), Iron 9%, Zinc 4%.

Canada's Food Guide Serving:

1 🌾 1½ 🥕

(279)

Lemon Chocolate Tart

This amazing pie is genuinely magical. During baking, some of the bottom chocolate crust rises to the top, leaving a lemon layer in the middle.

2 cups	chocolate wafer crumbs	500 mL
2 tbsp	butter, melted	25 mL
2 tbsp	corn syrup	25 mL
Lemon Filling:		
3	eggs	3
2	egg whites	2
3/4 cup	granulated sugar	175 mL
	Grated rind of 2 medium lemons	
1/2 cup	fresh lemon juice	125 mL
2 tsp	icing sugar	10 mL

1 In food processor, pulse chocolate wafer crumbs until fine. Mix butter with corn syrup. With machine running, drizzle butter mixture into crumbs, processing until mixed. Spray 9-inch (23 cm) pie plate or flan pan with nonstick cooking spray. Using hands or back of large spoon, spread chocolate mixture over bottom and up sides, pressing firmly so mixture holds together. Bake in 375°F (190°C) oven for 10 minutes.

2 Lemon Filling: In bowl, whisk together eggs, egg whites and sugar until well mixed. Whisk in lemon rind and juice. Pour into baked chocolate crust. Bake in 375°F (190°C) oven for 18 to 20 minutes or until top is barely set. Let cool.

3 Just before serving, sift icing sugar over top. *Makes 8 servings.*

Make ahead: Through step 1, let stand for up to 1 day. Through step 2, cover and refrigerate for up to 6 hours.

Per serving:

calories	278
protein	5 g
total fat	9 g
saturated fat	4 g
cholesterol	96 mg
carbohydrate	45 g
dietary fiber	1 g
sodium	109 mg

R.D.I. Vit A 8%, D 7%, E 8%, C 12%, Folate 5%, Ca 3% (30 mg), Iron 8%, Zinc 5%.

Canada's Food Guide Serving:
½)

Strawberries with Lemon Cream in Phyllo Pastry Cups

*Superb with strawberries, this dessert can show off other fruit, too.
I often use seasonal treats such as blueberries and mango, and even a combination of
berries. I garnish each cup with a fresh mint leaf or sometimes
pour a little Strawberry Sauce (page 269) over each.*

4	sheets phyllo pastry	4
4 tsp	butter, melted	20 mL
3/4 cup	light tub cream cheese	175 mL
1/3 cup	1% or 2% plain yogurt	75 mL
3 tbsp	granulated sugar	50 mL
	Finely grated rind of 1 lemon	
3 cups	sliced strawberries	750 mL
1 tbsp	icing sugar	15 mL

1 Lay one sheet of phyllo on work surface, keeping remainder covered with a damp tea towel to prevent drying out. Brush with 1 tsp (5 mL) of the butter. Using scissors, cut crosswise into three 5-inch (12 cm) wide strips; fold each strip into thirds to form square. Round off corners; gently mold into muffin cups. Repeat with remaining phyllo to make 12 cups. Bake in 400°F (200°C) oven for 5 minutes or until golden.

2 In bowl, mix together cream cheese, yogurt, sugar and lemon rind until smooth.

3 Divide filling among pastry cups; spoon strawberries over filling. Sift icing sugar over top. *Makes 6 servings, 2 each.*

Make ahead: Through step 1, store in airtight container at room temperature for up to 2 weeks. Through step 2, cover and refrigerate for up to 2 days. Fill shells just before serving.

Per tart:

calories	96
protein	3 g
total fat	4 g
saturated fat	2 g
cholesterol	11 mg
carbohydrate	12 g
dietary fiber	1 g
sodium	113 mg

R.D.I. Vit A 3%, E 2%, C 37%, Folate 5%, Ca 2% (21 mg), Iron 3%, Zinc 2%.

Canada's Food Guide Serving:
¼ 🌾 ½ 🥕

French Lemon Tart

It's hard to believe that something that tastes this good is so easy to make.
This is a lightened-up version of the traditional French tart au citron *with its thin,*
intense-flavored filling. I make the crust in a flan pan. If using a store-bought pie shell
or regular pie plate, reduce the volume of the filling by omitting the orange juice.

3	eggs	3
2	egg whites	2
3/4 cup	granulated sugar	175 mL
	Grated rind of 2 medium lemons	
1/2 cup	fresh lemon juice	125 mL
1/4 cup	fresh orange juice	50 mL
1	baked 9-inch (23 cm) pie shell (see Easy, No-Roll Food Processor Pastry, page 278)	1
2 tsp	icing sugar	10 mL

1 In bowl, using electric mixer, beat eggs, egg whites and sugar for 2 minutes or until creamy. Beat in lemon rind; continue beating and drizzle in lemon juice and orange juice. Place baked pie shell on baking sheet and fill with lemon mixture.

2 Bake in 350°F (180°C) oven for 25 to 30 minutes or until filling is slightly puffed, browned on top and barely set (may still wobble slightly in center). If necessary, cover with foil to prevent over-browning. Let cool completely.

3 Just before serving, sift icing sugar over top. *Makes 6 to 8 servings.*

Make ahead: Through step 2, cover and refrigerate for up to 8 hours.

Per serving:

calories	**249**
protein	**5 g**
total fat	**8 g**
saturated fat	4 g
cholesterol	96 mg
carbohydrate	**40 g**
dietary fiber	**I g**
sodium	**97 mg**

R.D.I. Vit A 9%, D 7%, E 4%, C 15%, Folate 6%, Ca 2% (18 mg), Iron 8%, Zinc 4%.

Canada's Food Guide Serving:

I 🌾 ½)

Xmas. Fruit Cake

½ cup. (half butter & half. marg)

¾ " sugar

¼ " corn syrup

½ tea sp. almond flavour

" " grated lemon & orange rind.

cups flour

tea sps bk powder.

tea sp. salt

eggs

cups sultanas

sps candied fruit
cherries pineapple

cup milk

can 11 by 4 "

ake at 325° for 1¾ hours.
ake brandy over top or glaze with warm corn syrup.

сир ни 65

2 | 84
10 | 92
29.   9 ½

2,0,4
247

Lemon Cheesecake with Raspberry Glaze

This cheesecake is so rich and creamy tasting that no one will believe how low it is in fat. Yogurt and cottage cheese replace some of the cream cheese called for in traditional recipes. Light cream cheese instead of regular reduces the fat further.

Cooking Tip

To prepare without a food processor or blender, press cottage cheese through sieve; beat with cream cheese until smooth. In large bowl, beat eggs and whites until foamy; beat in sugar. Add lemon rind and juice; sprinkle with flour. Add vanilla and yogurt mixture; beat until smooth.

2 cups	1% or 2% plain yogurt or 1 cup (250 mL) extra-thick yogurt	500 mL
2	medium lemons	2
1 cup	granulated sugar	250 mL
2 cups	1% or 2% cottage cheese	500 mL
8 oz	light cream cheese, cubed and softened	250 g
2	eggs	2
3	egg whites	3
1/4 cup	all-purpose flour	50 mL
1 tsp	vanilla	5 mL
Crust:		
1 cup	graham cracker crumbs	250 mL
1 tbsp	butter, melted	15 mL
2 tbsp	light corn syrup	25 mL
Raspberry Glaze:		
1	pkg (300 g) individually frozen raspberries, thawed*	1
4 tsp	cornstarch	20 mL
2 tbsp	icing sugar	25 mL
4 tsp	fresh lemon juice	20 mL

1 In cheesecloth-lined sieve set over bowl, drain plain yogurt (not extra-thick) in refrigerator for at least 3 hours or until reduced to 1 cup (250 mL). Discard liquid.
2 Spray bottom of 10-inch (3 L) springform pan with nonstick cooking spray or line with parchment paper. Center pan on foil; press foil to side of pan to keep water out when baking.

*If unavailable, substitute 1 pkg (425 g) frozen raspberries in light syrup; thaw and press through sieve. Use 1-1/3 cups (325 mL) of the juice.

Per serving:

calories	**268**
protein	**12 g**
total fat	**8 g**
saturated fat	**4 g**
cholesterol	**60 mg**
carbohydrate	**38 g**
dietary fiber	**1 g**
sodium	**373 mg**

R.D.I. Vit A 4%, D 3%, E 3%, C 13%, Folate 9%, Ca 12% (127 mg), Iron 6%, Zinc 8%.

Canada's Food Guide Serving:
½ 🌾 ¼ 🥕 ¼ 🥛

3 Crust: In food processor, mix crumbs with butter. Add corn syrup; process until mixture starts to hold together. Press evenly into bottom of pan. Bake in 350°F (180°C) oven for 10 minutes.

4 Grate rind from lemons and squeeze juice to make 1/2 cup (125 mL). In food processor, mix sugar, lemon juice and rind. Add cottage cheese; process until smooth, scraping down side of bowl. Add yogurt and cream cheese; process until smooth. Add eggs, egg whites, flour and vanilla; process until smooth. Pour over prepared crust.

5 Set springform pan in larger pan; pour in enough hot water to come halfway up side of springform pan. Bake in 325°F (160°C) oven for 1-1/4 hours or until set around edge yet still jiggly in center. Turn oven off; quickly run knife around cake. Let stand in oven for 1 hour.

6 Remove from larger pan and remove foil; let cool completely on rack. Cover and refrigerate for at least 2 hours or for up to 2 days.

7 Raspberry Glaze: In sieve set over bowl, drain raspberries, pressing berries to remove seeds and extract about 1-1/3 cups (325 mL) juice. In saucepan, whisk juice with cornstarch until smooth. Bring to boil over medium-high heat, stirring constantly; cook, stirring, until thickened and clear, about 1 minute. Stir in sugar and lemon juice; let cool. Pour evenly over cheesecake; refrigerate for at least 1 hour or until set. Remove side of pan. *Makes 12 servings.*

Make ahead: Through step 6, cover and refrigerate for up to 2 days. Through step 7, cover and refrigerate for up to 4 hours.

Lower-Fat Tip

Reduce the fat from dairy products (milk, yogurt, cottage cheese, sour cream) by choosing products with 1% or less fat.

Cooking Tip

Before adding raspberry glaze, line pan sides with 2 inch (5 cm) high waxed- or parchment-paper collar to prevent glaze from touching sides of pan. If it touches, discoloration may result.

Cranberry **Yogurt Flan**

*Tart cranberries add flavor, juiciness and color to this easy cheesecakelike
dessert, which is one of my favorites. It works just as tastily with blueberries or
raspberries instead of the cranberries.*

Cranberry Yogurt Squares
Prepare and bake as directed,
but use a 9-inch (2.5 L) square
cake pan; cut into squares.

Raspberry Yogurt Flan
Substitute 3 cups (750 mL)
fresh raspberries or 1 package
(300 g) individually frozen (not
thawed) for the cranberries.

Blueberry Yogurt Flan
Substitute 3 cups (750 mL)
fresh or frozen blueberries
(not thawed) for the
cranberries.

1-1/2 cups	all-purpose flour	375 mL
1/2 cup	granulated sugar	125 mL
1-1/2 tsp	baking powder	7 mL
1/3 cup	butter or soft margarine	75 mL
2	egg whites	2
1 tsp	vanilla	5 mL
2 cups	cranberries (fresh or frozen)	500 mL
Topping:		
2 tbsp	all-purpose flour	25 mL
2 cups	1% or 2% plain yogurt	500 mL
1	egg, lightly beaten	1
2/3 cup	granulated sugar	150 mL
2 tsp	grated lemon or orange rind	10 mL
1 tsp	vanilla	5 mL
2 tsp	icing sugar	10 mL

1 In food processor or bowl, combine flour, sugar, baking powder, butter, egg whites
and vanilla, mixing well. Press into bottom of lightly greased 10-inch (3 L) springform pan; sprinkle evenly with cranberries.

2 Topping: In bowl, sprinkle flour over yogurt. Add egg, sugar, lemon rind and vanilla;
mix until smooth. Pour over cranberries.

3 Bake in 350°F (180°C) oven for 60 to 70 minutes or until crust is golden. Serve
warm or cold. Sift icing sugar over top just before serving. *Makes 12 servings.*

Make ahead: Cover and refrigerate for up to 1 day.

Per serving:
calories	**227**
protein	**5 g**
total fat	**6 g**
saturated fat	**4 g**
cholesterol	**33 mg**
carbohydrate	**38 g**
dietary fiber	**1 g**
sodium	**129 mg**

R.D.I. Vit A 6%, D 1%, E 2%, C 3%,
Folate 4%, Ca 9% (95 mg), Iron 6%,
Zinc 6%.

Canada's Food Guide Serving:
¾ 🌾 ¼ 🥕 ¼ 🥛

Black Forest Frozen Yogurt Cake or Pie

All family members will love this frozen dessert. I particularly like the combination of frozen cherry and chocolate yogurt, but other flavors will taste fine, too.

2 tbsp	butter, melted	25 mL
2 tbsp	corn syrup	25 mL
1 tbsp	water	15 mL
1-1/2 cups	chocolate wafer cookie crumbs	375 mL
3 cups	chocolate frozen yogurt or ice cream	750 mL
2 cups	cherry frozen yogurt*	500 mL
1	can (14 oz/398 mL) pitted dark cherries	1
Cherry Sauce:		
4 tsp	cornstarch	20 mL
2 tbsp	fresh lemon juice	25 mL
2 tbsp	kirsch or black currant liqueur (cassis) or nectar	25 mL

1 In bowl, mix together butter, corn syrup and water; mix in crumbs. Firmly press into bottom and up sides of 9-inch (23 cm) pie plate or springform pan. Bake in 350°F (180°C) oven for 12 minutes; let cool. Freeze for 10 minutes or until firm.

2 Transfer chocolate and cherry frozen yogurt to refrigerator to soften slightly. Coarsely chop half of the cherries, reserving juice for sauce.

3 Working quickly, press frozen cherry yogurt into prepared crust. Sprinkle with chopped cherries. Press chocolate frozen yogurt on top, smoothing with spatula. Cover and freeze for 30 to 45 minutes or until firm.

4 Cherry Sauce: In saucepan, whisk reserved cherry juice with cornstarch; cook over medium-high heat, stirring constantly, until clear and thickened, about 2 minutes. Remove from heat. (Alternatively, in microwaveable dish, microwave on High for 2-1/2 minutes, stirring twice.) Stir in remaining cherries, lemon juice and liqueur; let cool. Pour over individual pieces of frozen cake when serving. *Makes 8 servings.*

Make ahead: Through step 3, cover and freeze for up to 1 week. Through step 4, cover and refrigerate sauce for up to 1 day.

Lower-Fat Tip

Light ice cream, frozen yogurts, sherbet and non-dairy frozen treats are good alternatives to regular and gourmet ice cream. Compare 1/2 cup (125 mL) of gourmet ice cream at about 17 grams of fat to a gourmet frozen yogurt at 2 grams of fat.

Cooking Tip

To make chocolate crumbs; process cookies in food processor.

* Substitution Tip

If cherry frozen yogurt isn't available, you can substitute strawberry, raspberry or vanilla.

Per serving:

calories	342
protein	7 g
total fat	9 g
saturated fat	4 g
cholesterol	20 mg
carbohydrate	60 g
dietary fiber	1 g
sodium	134 mg

R.D.I. Vit A 7%, E 6%, C 5%, Folate 8%, Ca 16% (179 mg), Iron 7%, Zinc 9%.

Canada's Food Guide Serving:

¼ 🥕 ½ 🍞

Orange Mousse Meringue Pie

Rich tasting and luscious, this pie is light because of its meringue crust and whipped evaporated milk filling. Be sure the evaporated milk is well chilled in order for it to whip.

3	egg whites	3
1/4 tsp	cream of tartar	1 mL
2/3 cup	granulated sugar	150 mL
1 tbsp	cornstarch	15 mL
Orange Mousse Filling:		
1	pkg (7 g) unflavored gelatin	1
	Grated rind of 2 medium oranges	
1-1/2 cups	fresh orange juice	375 mL
2	egg yolks	2
1/2 cup	granulated sugar	125 mL
3/4 cup	chilled 2% evaporated milk	175 mL

1 In bowl, beat egg whites with cream of tartar until soft peaks form. Gradually beat in sugar, 1 tbsp (15 mL) at a time, until stiff glossy peaks form. Blend in cornstarch.

2 Line baking sheet with parchment paper or foil; spread meringue into 9-inch (23 cm) circle, forming 1-inch (2.5 cm) high rounded rim. Bake in 300°F (150°C) oven for 1 hour or until lightly golden and crisp. Turn oven off; let meringue stand in oven for 12 hours. Gently peel off paper; place on serving plate.

3 Orange Mousse Filling: Sprinkle gelatin over 1/2 cup (125 mL) of the orange juice; set aside. In nonaluminum saucepan, whisk egg yolks lightly; add remaining orange juice, orange rind and sugar. Cook over medium heat, stirring constantly, for 5 to 10 minutes or until mixture thickens slightly and coats back of metal spoon. Remove from heat. Stir in gelatin mixture until dissolved. Cover and refrigerate for about 15 minutes or until thickened slightly.

4 In separate bowl, beat chilled evaporated milk until thickened and foamy, about 1 minute; fold into gelatin mixture until combined. Spoon into meringue pie shell; refrigerate for about 30 minutes or until set or for up to 8 hours. *Makes 8 servings.*

Make ahead: Through step 2, store in cardboard box or tin at room temperature for up to 1 week.

Fat-Reducing Tip

This evaporated milk has 2% b.f. (butterfat), yet provides the thickness and creaminess of regular 18% b.f. cream and double the amount of calcium.

Serving Tip

For a truly glamorous look, garnish the pie with twists of orange, mint sprigs and a dusting of cocoa powder.

Per serving:

calories	186
protein	5 g
total fat	2 g
saturated fat	1 g
cholesterol	57 mg
carbohydrate	38 g
dietary fiber	1 g
sodium	51 mg

R.D.I. Vit A 5%, D 15%, E 1%, C 43%, Folate 6%, Ca 8% (83 mg), Iron 3%, Zinc 4%.

Canada's Food Guide Serving:
¼ 🥕 ¼ 🍗

Dietary Help for Irritable Bowels

Irritable Bowel Syndrome (IBS) affects some 20% of otherwise healthy Canadians. Sufferers typically experience abdominal pain that is relieved with a bowel movement; alternating bouts of constipation with explosive diarrhea; and gas and bloating. Although there is no known cause or cure for IBS, diet can help control the symptoms. Since people respond differently to the changes suggested here, think of this advice as a starting point and be prepared to fine-tune it to suit yourself.

HEALTHY EATING TIPS: Irritable Bowels

- Keep a daily food journal. Look for links between foods eaten and onset of symptoms and eliminate suspect foods one at a time.
- Improve your eating habits overall. Eat 4 to 5 lower-fat meals and snacks, spaced regularly throughout the day.
- Fiber is a regulator, good for both diarrhea and constipation. Gradually increase your fiber intake by eating more whole grain foods, vegetables, fruit and legumes. Expect to suffer more from gas and bloating at first but this reaction shouldn't continue beyond a couple of months.

- If constipation is severe, add 1 tbsp (15 mL) of natural wheat bran to your diet each day, gradually increasing this to 3 to 4 tbsp (45 to 60 mL) daily over the next few months. Since bran works by absorbing moisture, drink 1 to 2 glasses of water along with the bran-containing food.
- If you suffer from diarrhea, choose foods high in soluble fiber such as oat bran, oatmeal, barley, legumes if tolerated, apples, applesauce, citrus fruits, psyllium-containing breakfast cereal; avoid foods containing the sweeteners sorbitol or mannitol; cut down on or eliminate caffeine-containing beverages, alcohol and spices.
- If excessive gas and bloating persist, try the suggestions given on page 128. Also consider eliminating lactose, the natural sugar in milk, by using lactose-reduced milk (sold alongside other milks) and avoiding processed cheese. Aged cheese and yogurt are low in lactose and shouldn't bother you.

Notes on Ingredients

Balsamic vinegar: This dark, rich-flavored, slightly sweet, mellow vinegar from Italy is available in supermarkets. If necessary, you can substitute 1 tbsp (15 mL) red wine vinegar plus a pinch of sugar for 1 tbsp (15 mL) balsamic vinegar.

Black bean sauce: A sauce, which is made from fermented black beans, is used in Chinese seafood, meat, poultry and vegetable dishes. It is available bottled in Asian grocery stores and the specialty section of supermarkets. I prefer the whole bean sauce to the purée.

Cheese: The fat content of cheese is listed on the label as a percentage of butter fat (b.f.) or milk fat (m.f.). This number indicates the percent of fat by weight and should not be confused with percent of calories from fat. Cheese labeled "light" is not necessarily a low-fat food. The term means simply that the cheese has at least 25% less fat than the regular kind. I often use the light Provolone-style cheese(12%) and the cheeses that are naturally lower in fat such as danbo at 9 to 13%, feta at 15 to 22% and creamy goat cheese (chèvre) 15 to 20%. Quark is a smooth, creamy, unripened soft cheese at 1 to 7%.

Chili paste or hot chili sauce: This red sauce, used in Asian cooking, is made from hot chili peppers, garlic and salt. A little goes a long way. It keeps well in the refrigerator for months. You can substitute hot pepper sauce.

Chinese noodles: Vacuum-packed, fresh Chinese wheat noodles (sometimes called chow mein noodles) are available in the vegetable section of many supermarkets. Some brands keep for at least 2 weeks in the refrigerator and are a great convenience food since they cook in boiling water in 2 to 3 minutes. If unavailable use Italian egg noodles. Rice noodles, usually dried, come in a variety of shapes, including rice vermicelli which are very thin. Soak rice noodles in warm water for 15 minutes then drain and use in soups or stir-frys. Cellophane (bean thread) noodles are made from ground mung beans. Soak 5 minutes in warm water before using.

Coconut milk: Coconut milk is a blend of freshly grated coconut and boiling water. It is used in soups, curries and sauces and is a staple in Thai cooking. Canned, light coconut milk has 12 to 20 grams of fat per cup; the regular kind is 75% higher in fat. Stir canned coconut milk well before using. Powdered coconut milk has an excellent flavor and is easy to use. However, it has about 4 grams fat per 1 tbsp (15 mL) powder. You can make your own light version by mixing less powder than called for with the water. For example, if you mix 5 tbsp (75 mL) powder with 1 cup (250 mL) water,

you will have 20 grams fat. Don't confuse coconut milk with sweetened coconut cream, which is used mainly for desserts and drinks, or with coconut water, the liquid inside a coconut.

Curry paste: Bottled or packaged Thai and Indian curry pastes are available in some supermarkets and specialty stores. They are a blend of spices, seasonings, vinegar and, sometimes, chili peppers. Use the paste in place of curry powder for a fresh flavor. Experiment with the pastes available; they vary widely in hotness and flavor. Pastes bought in a jar keep for months in the refrigerator.

Fish sauce: A staple in Thai cooking, fish sauce lends a salty fish flavor to dishes. You can sometimes substitute soy sauce but fish sauce has more flavor. All bottled fish sauce is high in sodium, although the amount varies widely from one brand to another. If you are concerned about sodium, look for brands with nutrition information on the label and choose the one lower in sodium. I use one that is lower than most yet has 760 mg sodium per 1 tbsp (15 mL). Fish sauce keeps in the cupboard for at least a year.

Five-spice powder: This fragrant pungent seasoning is a mixture of star anise, Szechuan peppercorns, fennel, cloves and cinnamon. It is found in the spice section of many supermarkets and in Chinese grocery stores. It keeps indefinitely in a sealed jar and is used in marinades and sauces.

Gingerroot: Fresh gingerroot adds wonderful flavor to vegetables, salads, sauces, marinades and stir-frys. Buy smooth, shiny, firm, not shriveled or moldy, gingerroot. Peel the ginger with a vegetable peeler or paring knife. Store in the refrigerator. It can also be frozen. Dried powdered ginger is a poor substitute.

Herbs: Use fresh herbs if possible. When buying dried herbs, choose the leaf not the powdered form. When substituting fresh for dried herbs, a rough guide is to use about 1 tbsp (15 mL) chopped fresh for 1 tsp (5 mL) dried leaf form. For basil or dill, I use 2 to 4 tbsp (25 to 50 mL) chopped fresh for 1 tsp (5 mL) dried. To store fresh herbs, wrap the roots or cut ends in a damp paper towel, refrigerate in a zip-lock bag. Wash herbs just before using.

Hoisin sauce: Widely used in Chinese cooking, Hoisin sauce is made from soybeans, vinegar, sugar and spices and is available in Asian markets and most supermarkets. Use this dark, sweet sauce in stir-frys, marinades or pasta sauces. Or spread over salmon, chicken or pork chops before grilling. It keeps in the refrigerator for months.

Italian seasoning: Premixed Italian seasoning is a convenience. To make your own, mix 1/2 tsp (2 mL) dried oregano, 3/4 tsp (4 mL) dried basil, a large pinch each of thyme, rosemary and marjoram.

Oyster sauce: Made from oysters and soy sauce but without a fishy taste, this thick, brown sauce is used in Chinese dishes. It is available bottled in Chinese grocery stores and some supermarkets. It will keep indefinitely in the refrigerator.

Rice: There are many kinds of rice. Brown rice is the most nutritious because it is whole grain and contains the bran. White rice, the most common, has had the bran removed during processing. Instant or pre-cooked rice is white rice that has been cooked then dehydrated. Parboiled or converted rice has been processed to force the nutrients from the bran into the center (the endosperm) of the rice. It is more nutritious than white rice. Basmati rice from India and Pakistan and jasmine rice from Thailand are long-grain rices with a fragrant nut-like aroma and flavor. Arborio rice is a short- to medium-grain rice imported from Italy used in risotto. (See page 116 for cooking instructions.)

Saffron: This most expensive of all spices is the rust-colored stigmas of a small crocus. Because of its strong aromatic flavor it is used in small amounts and should not be combined with other strong spices or herbs. For the most flavor, steep the threads in a small amount of hot water before adding to a dish. Buy saffron threads from Spain in small amounts rather than the powder, which tends to lose its flavor. Instead of saffron you can use turmeric to produce the bright yellow color; however, the flavor will be different.

Salt: When a recipe calls for "salt to taste," the amount of sodium in the salt is not included in the amount of sodium per serving given in the recipe's nutrition information box. If you add 1/2 tsp (2 mL) salt, you will add about 1200 mg sodium to the total recipe. Divide the amount by the number of servings to give you the added sodium per serving.

Sesame oil: This dark, nutty-flavored oil made from roasted sesame seeds is used for seasoning not as a cooking oil. It is usually added at the end of cooking and is delicious in stir-frys. Look for bottled sesame oil from Japan as North American brands are less flavorful. I don't use "light" sesame oil, which is light in color and flavor not in fat or calories.

Sodium: See Salt.

Soy sauce: This staple in Asian cooking is made from soy beans, salt and water. Reduced sodium soy sauce can be used in all recipes, but in some you may want to adjust the seasonings. One brand of "lite" or sodium-reduced soy sauce has 100 mg of sodium per 1/2 tsp (2 mL) soy sauce, which is 40% less sodium than the regular.

Vegetable oil: Most recipes call for "vegetable oil" rather than a specific oil such as canola or safflower because either works well in the recipe and we need a variety of fats in our diet. (For information on the types of fats in oils and their effect on health see the Appendix on page 292.) For a general all-purpose oil I use canola oil, which is very bland in flavor and lowest in saturated fat. For salad dressings and pasta sauces and for a stronger flavor, I use extra virgin olive oil. I don't buy bottles labeled "vegetable oil" unless the label also specifies the type of vegetable oil. I don't use "light" oils because they are light in color and flavor not in fat and calories.

Wasabi: Often called Japanese horseradish, wasabi is made from the root of an Asian plant. It is the hot green paste used in sushi and is available in either paste or powder form in Japanese markets or Asian food stores. To use the powder, mix with a small amount of water.

Yogurt cheese or drained yogurt: Yogurt cheese has a thick creamy texture and is a substitute for higher-fat dairy products such as sour cream or cream cheese in spreads and dips. When mixed with sugar, it is a delicious substitute for a whipped cream topping. To drain yogurt, place plain, low-fat yogurt made without gelatin in a cheesecloth-lined sieve set over a bowl (or use a yogurt drainer or coffee-filter sieve) and refrigerate for 6 hours or until about half the volume remains. For a thicker spread, drain for up to 48 hours. You can substitute extra-thick yogurt, available in some supermarkets, or some varieties of Greek-style yogurts.

Zest: The outermost layer of citrus fruits, mainly oranges or lemons, zest is removed with a zester (see photo page 276), paring knife or vegetable peeler. (Be sure to remove only the yellow or orange layer not the bitter white pith.) Zest contains aromatic oils which add intense flavor to sweet or savory dishes.

Appendix: Types of Fat

Some types of fat are better for you than others. The characteristic of each type and its effect on your health are largely determined by the fat's fatty acid makeup.

Fatty acids are chains of carbon and hydrogen atoms that form the basic building blocks of fat. The length of the carbon chain and the bonds between the carbon and hydrogen molecules determine the physical and chemical properties of each type of fat and its effect on your health.

Saturated fat is saturated because the fatty acids that make it up are fully loaded with hydrogen. Unsaturated fat, on the other hand, contains fatty acids that can still take on more hydrogen. Adding hydrogen to unsaturated fat is what hydrogenation is all about. An unsaturated liquid oil is made into a solid and saturated-like fat by adding hydrogen. The process changes the physical and chemical properties of the original fat as well as its health effects.

Polyunsaturated Fat (PUF or PUFA)
Two major kinds:
Omega-3 fat: eicosapentenoic (EPA) and docosahexanoic (DHA)
- linked to heart health
- shows anti-inflammatory effect in arthritis
Found mainly in
- fatty fish such as mackerel, herring, salmon, swordfish, trout, cod, bluefish

Omega-6 fat: linoleic acid
- use in small amounts as a source of an essential fatty acid
- linked to heart health but also to increased cancer risk when consumed in large amounts.
Found mainly in
- oils: safflower, sunflower, corn
- margarine made from these oils
- nuts, seeds

Monounsaturated Fat (MUF or MUFA)
- use in small amounts
- linked to heart health
Found mainly in
- oils: olive, canola, peanut
- margarine made with these oils
- nuts and seeds

Saturated Fat (SF or SFA)
- limit as much as possible
- linked to increased risk of heart disease
Found mainly in
- meat, poultry
- milk, cheese, yogurt, except skim milk products
- butter, lard
- palm, palm kernel, coconut oil

Trans fat (TF or TFA)
- avoid as much as possible
- increases risk of heart disease
Found in
- partially hydrogenated vegetable oils such as shortening
- hard, brick margarines

About the Nutrient Analysis

Nutrient analysis of the recipes was performed by Info Access (1988) Inc., Don Mills, Ontario, using the nutritional accounting system component of the CBORD Menu Management System. The nutrient database was the 1997 Canadian Nutrient File supplemented when necessary with documented data from reliable sources.

The analysis was based on:

- imperial measure and weights (except for foods typically packaged and used in metric quantity),
- smaller ingredient quantity when there was a range and
- the first ingredient listed when there was a choice.

Recipes were analyzed using canola vegetable oil, 1% milk, canned chicken broth and fish sauce containing 765 mg sodium per tablespoon (15 mL). Calculations of meat and poultry recipes assumed that only the lean portion was eaten.

Optional ingredients and ingredients in unspecified amounts (including salt to taste) were not included in the analysis. (Note 1/4 tsp /1mL salt contributes approximately 600 mg sodium.)

Nutrient values were rounded to the nearest whole number with non-zero values of 0.49 and less appearing as "trace." Selected vitamins and minerals* are presented as percentages of Recommended Daily Intakes (RDI) established for labeling purposes (*Guide to Food Labelling and Advertising, March 1996,* Agriculture and Agri-Food Canada). The RDIs are a reference standard developed for use in the nutrition labeling of foods in Canada. They reflect the highest recommended intake of each nutrient for each age/sex group, omitting supplemental needs for pregnancy and lactation.

Canada's Food Guide Servings

Canada's Food Guide to Healthy Eating contains daily serving recommendations for foods from four groups (grain products, vegetables and fruit, milk products, and meat and alternatives) and displays serving sizes for selected items. The number of Canada's Food Guide servings contributed by each recipe portion was calculated using custom software developed by Info Access. For items with variable Canada's Food Guide serving size, calculations were based on 50 grams of meat, poultry or fish, 1 egg and 1/2 cup (125 mL) canned or cooked dried legumes. Serving sizes for ingredients not specifically mentioned in Canada's Food Guide were approximated with reference to serving size and nutrient contribution of other foods in the same food group. Canada's Food Guide servings were rounded to quarter servings.

*Minerals and vitamins reported are those that are low in the diets of some Canadians (calcium, iron, zinc and folate) and others of widespread interest (vitamins A, D, E and C). B vitamins other than folate are not reported because they are prevalent in a variety of foods that Canadians regularly consume.

Daily Nutrient Values

The nutrient analysis that accompanies each recipe in this book tells you how much of each nutrient a serving or portion of that recipe contains. To find out how much of each nutrient you need on a daily basis, refer to the charts on this page. The values given here are general guidelines for healthy adults and do not reflect special additions or restrictions some people may require — for example, sodium restriction or extra iron to treat iron-deficiency anemia. Unless otherwise noted, these recommendations reflect Canada's Nutrition Recommendations, 1990.

mg = milligrams   mcg = micrograms   RE = Retinol Equivalents   I.U. = International Units

Age	Sex	Energy[1] (calories)	Protein (grams)	Carbohydrate[2] (grams)	Fiber[3] (grams)	Fat[4] 25% (grams)	Fat 30% (grams)	Cholesterol (mg)	Sodium[5] (mg)
19-24	Males	3000	61	413	25-35	83	100	300 or less	2000 or less
	Females	2100	50	289	25-35	58	70	300 or less	2000 or less
25-49	Males	2700	64	371	25-35	75	90	300 or less	2000 or less
	Females	1900	51	261	25-35	53	63	300 or less	2000 or less
50-74	Males	2300	63	316	25-35	64	77	300 or less	2000 or less
	Females	1800	54	248	25-35	50	60	300 or less	2000 or less
75 +	Males	2000	59	275	25-35	56	67	300 or less	2000 or less
	Females	1700	55	234	25-35	47	57	300 or less	2000 or less

VITAMINS

Age	Sex	A[6] (includes Beta Carotene) RE (I.U.)	D[7] mcg (I.U.)	E mg (I.U.)	C[8] (mg)	Folic Acid[9] mcg (mg)	Calcium[10] (mg)	Iron (mg)	Zinc (mg)
19-24	Males	1000 (5700)	5 (200)	10 (16)	40	220 (.22)	1000	9	12
	Females	800 (4600)	5 (200)	7 (12)	30	180 (.18)	1000	13	9
25-49	Males	1000 (5700)	5 (200)	9 (15)	40	230 (.23)	1000	9	12
	Females	800 (4600)	5 (200)	6 (10)	30	185 (.19)	1000	13	9
			(up to age 70)						
50-74	Males	1000 (5700)	10 (400)	7 (12)	40	230 (.23)	1200	9	12
	Females	800 (4600)	10 (400)	6 (10)	30	195 (.20)	1200	8	9
			(age 71 +)						
75 +	Males	1000 (5700)	15 (600)	6 (10)	40	215 (.22)	1200	9	12
	Females	800 (4600)	15 (600)	5 (8)	30	200 (.20)	1200	8	9

[1] Calories are based on the energy needs of a moderately active, average person.

[2] Carbohydrate values have been calculated based on the nutrition recommendation that approximately 55% of the days' calories should come from carbohydrate. This includes both starch and sugar.

[3] Fiber values represent a daily fiber intake generally recognized as necessary for good health.

[4] Fat values are based on fat providing 25% or 30% of the day's calories. The former value is commonly used for cholesterol-lowering diets. The latter represents a goal for general, healthy eating.

[5] The sodium value represents practical healthy eating advice set at the mid-range of advice that ranges from 1800-2300 mg a day.

[6] Vitamin A includes beta carotene; preformed vitamin A is found only in foods of animal origin, whereas beta carotene comes primarily from plant sources.

[7] Vitamin D values are taken from the 1997 recommendations of the National Academy of Sciences.

[8] Vitamin C intakes should increase by 50% for smokers.

[9] Folic acid values reflect what you need to get to meet basic nutrition requirements, not extra amounts recommended to prevent neural tube defects.

[10] Calcium values are taken from the 1997 recommendations of the National Academy of Sciences.

Canadian Diabetes Association Food Choice Value

The Canadian Diabetes Association Food Choice Values contained in the following table are part of the Good Health Eating Guide system of meal planning (1998). This system is based on Canada's Food Guide to Healthy Eating. A dietitian can tailor the meal plan to meet individual needs.

People using the Good Health Eating Guide system can see how to fit recipes into their personalized meal plan. Some recipes may exceed the recommended number of servings on the meal plan at a particular meal. These can be incorporated by reducing the portion size.

Nutrient values displayed with the recipes in this book have been rounded to the nearest whole number. Canadian Diabetes Association Food Choice Values have been assigned on the basis of nutrient values rounded to one decimal point.

For more information on diabetes, the Good Health Eating Guide or the Canadian Diabetes Association, please contact: The Canadian Diabetes Association National Office, Suite 800, 15 Toronto Street, Toronto, Ontario M5C 2E3. 1-800-Banting (226-8464) or on the World Wide Web at www.diabetes.ca.

The following Canadian Diabetes Association Food Choice Values refer to the main recipe indicated, not to recipe variations that may appear on those pages.

		FOOD CHOICE VALUE PER SERVING						
Page		STARCH ▫	FRUITS & VEGETABLES ◪	MILK ◆	SUGARS ✴	PROTEIN ⦸	FATS & OILS ▲	EXTRA ▣
Appetizers								
8	Grilled Quesadillas: Avocado 1/8 of recipe	1 1/2	1/2			1/2	1 1/2	
9	Shrimp Quesadillas 1 wedge (1/24 of recipe)	1/2				1/2		
10	Mini Phyllo Tart Shells 1 tart (1/36 of recipe)							1
11	Mango Salsa in Mini Phyllo Tarts 1 tart (1/30 of recipe)							1
12	Spicy Hummus 3 tbsp (1/16 of recipe)		1/2					
13	Caramelized Onion and Basil Dip 2 tbsp (1/25 of recipe)		1/2					
14.	Creamy Crab Dip 2 tbsp (1/20 of recipe)					1/2		
15	Black Bean Dip with Veggie Topping 2 tbsp (1/16 of recipe)		1/2					
20	Creamy Coriander Mint Dip 2 tbsp (1/13.3 of recipe)			1/2 1%				
21	Smoked Trout Spread: Yogurt 2 tbsp (1/13.3 of recipe)					1/2		
22	Herbed Yogurt-Cheese 2 tbsp (1/8 of recipe)			1/2 1%				
23	Mushroom Bruschetta 1 piece (1/12 of recipe)	1/2				1/2	1/2	1
24	Marinated Mussels 1/45 of recipe							1
28	Crab Cakes 1/6 of recipe	1/2				3		1
29	Spiced Shrimp 3 pieces (1/13.3 of recipe)					1		
30	Hoisin Smoked-Turkey Spirals 2 pieces (1/20 of recipe)	1/2				1/2		
31	Sesame Wasabi Spirals with light mayonnaise 2 pieces 1/20 of recipe	1/2					1/2	
32	Roasted Red Pepper and Arugula Spirals 2 pieces (1/20 of recipe)	1/2					1/2	

Page		STARCH	FRUITS & VEGETABLES	MILK	SUGARS	PROTEIN	FATS & OILS	EXTRA
32	Smoked Salmon and Cream Cheese Spirals							
	Yogurt Cheese 2 pieces (1/20 of recipe)	1/2				1/2		
	Herbed Light Cream Cheese 2 pieces (1/20 of recipe)	1/2				1/2	1/2	
33	Teriyaki Chicken Bites 1/24 of recipe					1/2		
35	Citrus Mint Iced Tea 1/6 of recipe		1/2		1			

Salads

Page		STARCH	FRUITS & VEGETABLES	MILK	SUGARS	PROTEIN	FATS & OILS	EXTRA
38	Spinach Salad with Walnut Vinaigrette 1/8 of recipe						1	1
39	Carrot Slaw with Radicchio 1/4 of recipe		1				1	
40	Garlic Green Beans with Flavored Oil 1/8 of recipe		1/2				1/2	
41	Fresh Beet and Onion Salad 1/4 of recipe		1				1/2	
42	Watercress, Orange and Chick-Pea Salad 1/4 of recipe	1/2	1			1/2		
43	Indonesian Coleslaw 1/8 of recipe		1/2		1/2		1/2	
44	Thai Vegetarian Salad 1/4 of recipe		1			1	1/2	
45	Black Bean and Corn Salad 1/8 of recipe	1				1/2		1
46	Marinated Shrimp and Mango Salad 1/6 of recipe		2 1/2		1	4 1/2		
48	Arugula Salad with Grilled Chèvre 1/8 of recipe		1/2			1/2	1 1/2	
50	Curried Lentil, Wild Rice and Orzo Salad 1/8 of recipe	1 1/2	1/2			1/2	1 1/2	1
51	Chicken Penne Salad with Thai Dressing 1/6 of recipe	2	1/2			3 1/2		
53	Tomato and Corn Pasta Salad 1/8 of recipe	3 1/2				1	1	1
54	Pesto Pasta Salad with Chicken and Sun-Dried Tomatoes 1/6 of recipe	4				3		
55	Couscous, Orange and Carrot Salad 1/6 of recipe	2	2				1	
56	Yogurt Parsley Dressing 1 tbsp (1/26.7 of recipe)						1/2	
57	Herb and Ginger Vinaigrette 1 tbsp (1/8 of recipe)				1/2		1/2	

Soups

Page		STARCH	FRUITS & VEGETABLES	MILK	SUGARS	PROTEIN	FATS & OILS	EXTRA
60	Tortellini Vegetable Soup 1/4 of recipe	1 1/2	1/2			1 1/2	1/2	
61	Portuguese Chick-Pea and Spinach Soup 1/6 of recipe	1	1/2			1		
62	Soup au Pistou 1/6 of recipe	1	1			1 1/2	1/2	
63	Winter Vegetable Soup 1/4 of recipe	1	1			1/2	1	
66	Sweet Potato and Ginger Soup 1/8 of recipe	1 1/2					1	
67	Lightly Curried Carrot and Ginger Soup 1/6 of recipe		1	1/2 2 %			1/2	
68	Asian Carrot and Mushroom Noodle Soup 1/5 of recipe	1/2	1/2			1 1/2		
70	Spicy Thai Chicken Noodle Soup 1/6 of recipe	1				2		1
71	Chinese Shrimp and Scallop Soup 1/4 of recipe	1				1 1/2		
72	Thai Coconut, Ginger and Chicken Soup 1/4 of recipe	1/2				1	1/2	

Page		STARCH	FRUITS & VEGETABLES	MILK	SUGARS	PROTEIN	FATS & OILS	EXTRA
73	Porcini Mushroom Bisque 1/6 of recipe		1/2	1/2 2%			1/2	1
75	Lentil, Barley and Sweet Potato Soup 1/8 of recipe	1	1			1/2		
76	Mulligatawny Soup 1/6 of recipe		1 1/2			2 1/2		
77	Quick Black Bean, Corn and Tomato Soup 1/6 of recipe	1	1 1/2			1/2		
78	Onion and Potato Soup 1/8 of recipe	1/2	1/2			1/2	1/2	
79	Gazpacho 1/8 of recipe		1			1/2		

Pasta

Page		STARCH	FRUITS & VEGETABLES	MILK	SUGARS	PROTEIN	FATS & OILS	EXTRA
82	Pasta with Chick-Peas and Spinach 1/3 of recipe	3 1/2				1 1/2		1
83	Easy Creamy Turkey Fettuccine 1/3 of recipe	3 1/2	1	1 1/2 2%		4		
84	Summer Corn and Tomato Pasta 1/10 of recipe	2				1/2	1	
85	Fettuccini with Pesto 1/4 of recipe	4 1/2				1	1 1/2	
87	Linguine with Shrimp and Fresh Basil 1/4 of recipe	4	1 1/2			3 1/2		
88	Pad Thai 1/4 of recipe	3	1		1/2	2 1/2	1	
90	Penne with Tomato, Tuna and Lemon 1/3 of recipe	3 1/2	1			2 1/2		
91	Thai Noodle and Vegetable Stir-Fry 1/4 of recipe	1 1/2	1/2			1/2	1	
92	Singapore-Style Noodles 1/4 of recipe	2	2			1 1/2	1	
93	Chinese Noodle and Shrimp Party Platter 1/10 of recipe	1 1/2	1			2 1/2		
96	Wild Mushroom and Spinach Lasagna 1/6 of recipe	2 1/2	1/2	1 1/2 1%		2 1/2	1/2	1
98	Grilled Italian Sausage and Red Peppers with Penne 1/4 of recipe	4	1 1/2			3	2	
99	Vegetable Tortellini Casserole with Cheese Topping 1/6 of recipe	3	2			2 1/2	1 1/2	
100	Penne with Sweet Red Peppers, Black Olives and Arugula 1/4 of recipe	3				1	2	1
102	Skillet Pork Curry with Apples and Chinese Noodles 1/6 of recipe	2	1 1/2	1/2 1%	1/2	4 1/2		
103	Lemon, Dill and Parsley Orzo 1/4 of recipe	2					1	
105	Beef, Tomato and Mushroom Rigatoni 1/6 of recipe	2 1/2	1 1/2			3		1
106	Spicy Chicken with Broccoli and Chinese Noodles 1/6 of recipe	1 1/2	1 1/2			4 1/2		
107	Two-Cheese Pasta and Tomatoes 1/6 of recipe	2 1/2	1/2			2	1/2	

Vegetarian Main Dishes

Page		STARCH	FRUITS & VEGETABLES	MILK	SUGARS	PROTEIN	FATS & OILS	EXTRA
111	Mediterranean Vegetable Stew 1/4 of recipe	2	1/2			1/2	1	
113	Vegetarian Paella 1/6 of recipe	4 1/2	2			1	1	1
115	Artichoke, Goat Cheese, Fresh Tomato and Onion Pizza 1/6 of recipe	2	1/2			1	1/2	
116	Leek and Rice Pilaf 1/4 of recipe	2 1/2					1	1
117	Potato Vegetable Curry 1/4 of recipe	1	1			1/2	1/2	
118	Sweet Potato, Squash and Bulgur Casserole 1/4 of recipe	1 1/2	2				1	
120	Mushroom Lentil Burgers 1/4 of recipe	1 1/2	1/2			1		

Page		STARCH	FRUITS & VEGETABLES	MILK	SUGARS	PROTEIN	FATS & OILS	EXTRA
121	Chick-Pea Burgers 1/4 of recipe	1 1/2	1/2			1/2	1/2	
123	Sunflower Veggie Tofu Burgers 1/4 of recipe	2	1/2			2	1	
124	Grilled Portobello Mushroom Burgers 1 burger (1/4 of recipe)	2	1/2			1 1/2	1 1/2	1
125	Coconut Rice 1/4 of recipe	2 1/2					1/2	1
126	Mexican Brown Rice with Tomatoes and Corn 1/4 of recipe	4	1 1/2				1	
127	Couscous with Tomato and Basil 1/4 of recipe	2	1/2				1/2	
129	Tuscan White Kidney Beans with Sage 1/4 of recipe	1				1		
130	Quinoa Pilaf 1/3 of recipe	1 1/2	1/2			1/2	1	
131	Tofu Vegetable Shish Kebabs 1/4 of recipe		1			1 1/2		
132	Lentil and Vegetable Curry 1/6 of recipe	1 1/2	1			1		
133	Barley and Black Bean Casserole 1/10 of recipe	2					1/2	

Vegetable Side Dishes

Page		STARCH	FRUITS & VEGETABLES	MILK	SUGARS	PROTEIN	FATS & OILS	EXTRA
136	Spanish-Style Asparagus 1/4 of recipe		1/2				1/2	
136	Roasted Asparagus with Parmesan 1/4 of recipe					1/2	1/2	1
137	Asparagus with Shaved Parmesan 1/4 of recipe		1/2			1/2		
137	Make-Ahead Cumin-Spiced Broccoli 1/4 of recipe		1/2			1/2	1/2	
138	Spiced Cabbage and Spinach 1/4 of recipe		1/2				1	
139	Spinach with Tomatoes and Cumin 1/3 of recipe		1/2				1/2	
140	Beet Greens with Lemon and Almonds 1/3 of recipe					1/2	1/2	1
141	Tomato Gratin 1/4 of recipe	1/2	1/2			1/2	1	
142	Tomatoes Provençal 1/6 of recipe		1/2				1/2	1
143	New Potatoes with Mint Pesto 1/6 of recipe	1					1/2	1
144	Sesame-Spiced Oven-Fried Potatoes 1/4 of recipe	2 1/2					1	
146	Herb-Roasted Potatoes and Onions 1/4 of recipe	1 1/2					1 1/2	
147	Skillet Sweet Potatoes 1/3 of recipe	2					1/2	
147	Carrots Provençal 1/4 of recipe		1				1/2	
148	Two-Potato Scallop 1/4 of recipe	3				1/2	1/2	
149	Broccoli Carrot Stir-Fry 1/4 of recipe		1 1/2				1	
150	Carrot and Squash Purée with Citrus 1/4 of recipe		1 1/2					
151	Braised Fennel with Parmesan 1/6 of recipe					1/2		1
154	Grilled Marinated Portobello Mushrooms 1/4 of recipe		1/2				1/2	
155	Roasted Eggplant Slices with Roasted Garlic Purée 1/4 of recipe		1/2				1	1
155	Roasted Garlic Purée 1/4 of recipe (1 tbsp)		1/2					
157	Roasted Winter Vegetables 1/8 of recipe	1/2	1 1/2				1	

Page		STARCH	FRUITS & VEGETABLES	MILK	SUGARS	PROTEIN	FATS & OILS	EXTRA
Meat and Poultry								
160	Ginger Chicken 1/4 of recipe		1/2			3 1/2		
161	Asian Chicken 1/6 of recipe				1/2	4		1
162	Mexican Chicken with Cumin and Garlic 1/4 of recipe					5		
163	Spicy Baked Chicken with Tomato Salsa 1/4 of recipe		1/2			5		
164	Thai Chicken Curry in Coconut Milk 1/4 of recipe		1			5		
165	Baked Chicken Breasts with Mango Chutney Sauce 1/4 of recipe				1 1/2	5 1/2		
168	Chicken, Italian Sausage and Sweet Pepper Skewers 1/6 of recipe		1			3 1/2		
170	Chicken, Spinach and Dried Cranberry Phyllo Pie 1/6 of recipe	1/2	1/2	1 2%		2 1/2	1	1
171	Sesame Herb Chicken 1/4 of recipe	1/2				5		
172	Provençal Saffron Chicken 1/8 of recipe		1 1/2			5		
173	Romaine Salad with Grilled Lemon Chicken 1/4 of recipe		1			4		
174	Roasted Chicken, Fennel and Sweet Potatoes 1/4 of recipe	2	1/2			1 1/2	1	
176	Cornish Hens with Porcini Mushroom and Basil Stuffing 1/6 of recipe	1/2	1/2			5		
178	Cranberry-Glazed Turkey Breast 1/6 of recipe				4	6		
179	Turkey Potato Patties 1/4 of recipe	1				1 1/2	1/2	
180	Grilled Turkey Scaloppini in Citrus Ginger Sauce 1/4 of recipe		1			4		
181	Turkey Scaloppini with Tomato and Herbs 1/4 of recipe		1/2			4		1
182	Ginger Beef and Broccoli Stir-Fry 1/4 of recipe		1			4		
183	Szechuan Green Beans and Beef with Rice 1/4 of recipe	3 1/2	1 1/2		1/2	1 1/2	1/2	
184	Salsa Meat Loaf 1/4 of recipe	1/2	1/2			3 1/2		
185	Picadillo 1/5 of recipe		2 1/2			2 1/2	1/2	
186	Beef Fajitas 1/4 of recipe	2 1/2	1			2 1/2		
188	Mexican Pork Loin Roast 1/6 of recipe					4		
190	Chinese Barbecued Pork Tenderloin 1/6 of recipe				1/2	4		
191	Thai Pork and Vegetable Curry with Fresh Basil 1/4 of recipe	1	1/2			3 1/2	1/2	
192	Rack of Lamb with Wine Sauce 1/4 of recipe		1/2		1/2	3		
193	Cucumber Mint Raita 1/4 cup (1/4 of recipe)			1/2 1%				
195	Greek Marinated Leg of Lamb 1/10 of recipe					4 1/2		
Fish								
198	Hoisin-Glazed Sea Bass 1/4 of recipe				1/2	3		
199	Red Snapper with Lime Coriander Marinade 1/4 of recipe					5		
200	Monkfish with Sun-Dried Tomatoes, Capers and Basil 1/4 of recipe		1/2			4		
201	Oven-Fried Fish Fillets 1/4 of recipe	1/2				4		1

Index of Recipes

A

Almonds:
  beet greens with, 140
  salad, lentil, wild rice and orzo, 50
  soup, sweet potato and ginger, 66
  to toast, 50, 66
Antipasto platter, 29
Appetizers, 8-35. *See also* Dips; Spreads
  antipasto platter, 29
  bruschetta, mushroom, 23
  chicken, teriyaki bites, 33
  crab cakes, 28
  grilled,
    mushrooms, 154
    quesadillas, 8
  hummus, 12
  mini phyllo shells, 10, 11
    mango in, 11
  mussels, marinated, 24
  shrimp,
    quesadillas, 9
    spiced, 29
  spirals,
    red pepper and arugula, 32
    sesame wasabi, 31
    smoked salmon and cream cheese, 32
    smoked turkey, 30
Apple(s):
  cake, cranberry, 263
  cobbler, strawberry, 272
  crisp, 271
  curry, pork tenderloin, 102-3
  pie, apricot deep-dish, 277
Applesauce, raisin spice loaf, 249
Apricot:
  pie, apple deep-dish, 277
  raspberry parfait, 273
Artichoke(s):
  paella, 113-14
  pizza, goat cheese, tomato and onion, 115
Arugula:
  pasta, with sweet red peppers and black olives, 100
  salad,
    with grilled chèvre, 48
    orange and chick-pea, 42
    shrimp and mango, 46-7
    tomato and red onion, 57
  spirals, red pepper, 32
Asian-style:
  chicken, 161
    barbecued, 161
  soup, carrot and mushroom noodle, 68
Asparagus:
  and mushroom gratin, 224
  roasted, with Parmesan, 136
  with shaved Parmesan, 137
  Spanish-style, 136
Avocado:
  fajitas, beef, 186
  quesadillas, grilled, 8
  sandwich, cheese focaccia, 230

B

Balsamic vinegar:
  about, 290
  vinaigrette, 39
Bamboo shoots, Chinese shrimp and scallop soup, 71
Bananas:
  cupcakes, chocolate, 255
  muffins, strawberry-glazed pineapple, 243
Barbecue(d):
  See also Grilled
  chicken, Asian-style, 161
  pork tenderloin, Chinese-style, 190
Barley:
  casserole, black bean and, 133
  soup, lentil and sweet potato, 75
Basil:
  chicken, teriyaki bites, 33
  couscous with tomato and, 127
  dressing, yogurt, 56
  linguine with shrimp and, 87
  pesto sauce, 85
  soup au pistou, 62
  substitute, 13, 62, 83, 98
Beans:
  See also Black beans; Green beans; Kidney beans
  pinto, dip with veggie topping, 15
  soup,
    au pistou, 62
    pasta, au pistou, 62
Bean sprouts:
  Indonesian coleslaw, 43
  noodles, 92
    and shrimp platter, 93
  pad Thai, 88
  soup, chicken noodle, 70
Beef:
  See also Hamburger
  about, 187
  ground,
    fajitas, 186
    and green beans with rice, 183
    meat loaf, 184
    picadillo, 185
    tomato and mushroom rigatoni, 105
  steak, fajitas, 186
  stir-fry, and broccoli, 182
Beet greens:
  See also Greens
  with lemon and almonds, 140
Beet(s):
  burgers, sunflower veggie tofu, 123
  pita wrap, tuna and veggie, 234
  to prepare and cook, 140
  salad, and onion, 41
  serving tip, 41
Beverages:
  cranberry spritzer, 237
  non-alcoholic,
    citrus mint iced tea, 35
    fruit smoothies, 35
    fruit spritzers, 35
Bisque, porcini mushroom, 73
Black beans:
  and barley casserole, 133
  dip with veggie topping, 15
  Mexican brown rice with tomatoes and, 126
  pasta, corn and tomato, 84
  salad,
    corn, 45
    pasta, tomato and corn, 53
    soup, corn and tomato, 77
Black bean sauce, about, 290
Black Forest frozen yogurt cake, 287
Blueberry(ies):
  cake, lemon coffee, 256
  and cantaloupe with strawberry sauce, 269
  crisp, apple, 271
  flan, yogurt, 286
  muffins, oat bran, 241
  pie, peach, 279
Bok choy, Chinese shrimp and scallop soup, 71
Bran muffins, 240, 241, 244
Bread:
  apple-raisin spice, 249
  bruschetta, 23
  fig and cottage cheese, 245
  focaccia, 246
  fruit soda, 248
Bread crumbs, homemade, 142, 176
Broccoli:
  chicken and Chinese noodles with, 106-7
  cumin-spiced, 137
  stir-fry,
    carrot, 149
    and ginger beef, 182
Brown rice. *See* Rice
Brunch, 219-37
Bruschetta, 23